Building English Vocabulary with Etymology
Introduction

Peter R. Beaven

Building English Vocabulary with Etymology
Introduction
Peter R. Beaven

Senior Editor:
Katherine Webster

Contributors:
Nicia Gruener, Stephen E. Stapczynski
Dominic M. Brown, S. James Boumil III

Revised August 28 2018

Published by
The Cheshire Press
an imprint of The Cheshire Group
Andover, MA 01810-0037
www.cheshirepress.com

All rights reserved. No part of this book may be reproduced or transmitted in any form or by any means without the express written consent of the author, except for the inclusion of quotations in reviews.

Copyright © 2005-2016 by Beaven & Associates

ISBN: 978-0-9824740-0-6

Library of Congress Control Number: 2016962689

Printed in the United States of America

Beaven & Associates
3 Dundee Park, #202
Andover, MA 01810
www.beavenandassociates.com

Beaven, Peter R.
Building English Vocabulary with Etymology
Introduction

Contents

Preface..5

Lesson I ....…....……..AB-, AC-, AMBI-,
                                    ANTE-, BENE-, BI-..7

Lesson II…………….........CIRCUM-, CO-, CONTRA-,
                                    DE-, DIS-, DUO- 13

Lesson III…………..…............EQUI-, EX-, EXTRA-,
                                    IN-, IL-, INTER-, INTRA-................................19

Lesson IV…………...........…...MAGNUS-, MAL-, MULTI-,
                                    OB-, OMNI-, PER-, POST- PRE-.....................24

Lesson V…...........................PRIM- PRO-, RE-, RETRO-, SE-,
                                    SUB-, SUPER-, TRANS-, UNI-........................30

Quiz 1..36

Lesson VI......................AC-, AG-, AGRI-, ALI-, ALT-, ALTI-, AMOR-,
                                    AMBUL-, ANIM-, ANNUS, APER-, APT-...............37

Lesson VII.......ARM-, ART-, AUD-, AVUNCULUS, BATTU-, BEATUS, BELLI,
                        BIB-, BREVE, CAD-, 68CALCITR-, CAND-, CANT-, CAP-.............42

Lesson VIII... CAPUT, CARN-, CASTIG-, CEREBRUM, CERN-, CED-, CELER,
                                    CENS-, CENT-, CID-, CIT-, CIVIS...................48

Lesson IX…………..CLAM-, CLAR-, CLAUD-, CLIN-, COGNIT-, COLLUM,
                                    COMPL-, COPIA, COR, CORPUS, CRED-.............54

Lesson X…................CRESC-, CRUCIS, CUMB-, CULPA, CUPI-, CURR-,
                                    DA-, DENS, DICT-, DOC-, DOMIN-..................61

Quiz 2..67

Lesson XI............…....DORMI-, DORSUM, EGO, EQU-, ERR-, FAC-, FACIES,
                                    FALL-, FER-, FERV-, FIDES, FINIS, FING-............68

Lesson XII…..........FIRMUS, FLECT-, FLORIS, FLU-, FORS, FORUM, FRANG-,
                                    FRATER, FRONS, FUG-, FUS-, GURG-, GEN-.........74

Lesson XIII….............GRAD-, GRAT-, GREGIS, HER-, IMPEL-, INCEND-,
                                    IRA, ITER, JAC-, JOCUS, JUDIC-, JUNCT-.............80

Lesson XIV... LABOR-, LATERAL, LAV-, LEGIS, LEVIS, LIBER, LICENCIA, LIGO,
LINGUA, LITTERA, LOCUS, LOQU-, LUCIS, LUD-..................86

Lesson XV........................MANUS, MAR, MATER, MEDIUS, MEM-,
MENDUM, MERG-, MINUS, MISS-, MOT-..........................92

Quiz 3..97

Lesson XVI............MON-, MONS, MOR-, MORI, MUT-, NAT-, NAVIS, NEG-,
NIHIL, NOMEN, NOV-, NOCT, NUNCIO..........................98

Lesson XVII...OCULUS, ODI-, OLE-, OPER-, ORA-, ORBIS, ORDO, ORN-, OSTEND-,
PASC-, PASS-, PATER, PAX, PECCATUM, PECUNIA, PEL-, PEND-, PED...104

Lesson XVIII.........PET-, PICTUS, PIUS, PLAC-, PON-, PONDUS, PONS, PORT-,
PORTUS, POTEN-, POT-, PRAEDA, PREHEND-..................110

Lesson XIX......................PRESS-, PUNG-, PUNI-, PUT-, RAP-, RATIO,
REC-, RID-, ROG-, ROTA, RUPT-..................116

Lesson XX....................SACR-, SALI-, SALIS, SANGUIS, SATIS, SCRIB-,
SECT-, SEQUI, SED-, SENSIS, SENS-..................122

Quiz 4..128

Lesson XXI..............................SIMI-L, SOLUS, SOLV-,
SOMN-, SON, SPARG-, SPEC-..........................129

Lesson XXII............SPIR-, STAT-, STELLA, STRICT-, STRUCT-, SUAVIS,
SUM-, TANG-, TEMPER-, TEMPOR-..........................135

Lesson XXIII.................TEN-, TERM-, TERR-, TEX-, TORS-, TOTUS,
TRACT-, TRUD-, TURB-, ULTIMA, UPT-, UND-..........................141

Lesson XXIV...............URBS, VAC-, VAD-, VAL-, VENDIC-, VENI-,
VENTUS, VER-, VERBUM, VERS-..........................146

Lesson XXV......................VIA, VID-, VIGIL-, VINC-,
VIT-, VOC-, VOL-, VOLV-..........................153

Quiz 5..159

Answer Key..160

Index..187

Etymology in Building English Vocabulary

The word "etymology" refers to tracing the origin and historical development of words in a language. How is a given word derived from an earlier word or words in a native or foreign language?

Just as we can "parse" or break up a sentence into parts of speech - noun, verb, adjective, adverb, etc. - so we can deconstruct a given word into its constituent meaning elements and trace their origins. For example, the word "etymology" consists of an original Greek root "etymon" - meaning "an earlier form of the same word" - and the Greek "logos" - meaning "word" or "speech", which took on the later form "-ology" - meaning "study of." So, there we have the etymology of the word "etymology."

Studying the etymology of vocabulary words reveals repeated word-formation patterns, so that we can dissect or guess the meanings of unfamiliar words based on their constituent prefixes and roots that we have encountered earlier. For example, by knowing that the prefix "pre-" means "before" or "ahead" and that "dict" is rooted in "speaking" or "saying," we can surmise that "predict" means to foretell or talk about something before it happens.

The English language is built primarily from the Anglo-Saxon (Germanic), Latin, and Greek languages. Historically, the Angles and Saxons drove out the original Celtic inhabitants and occupied Britain, and after a few brief occupations by the Roman legions, in 1066 the tribes were defeated by the Norman leader William the Conqueror, who spoke French - a language derived almost entirely from Latin. Over time, the Germanic and Latinate languages blended to become what we know as English.

Because Latin is such a fundamental basis of English and because Latin is built from a regular system of "reusable" prefixes and roots, studying these elements makes learning vocabulary more efficient. Instead of learning word meanings in isolation, by learning a standard set of Latin prefixes and common roots we can "mix and match" to learn several new words or variations. The study of etymology thus can accelerate the expansion of our vocabulary while helping us appreciate how meanings and usages have evolved.

For example, knowing that the root "gress" means "step" or "advance", and knowing a series of prefixes, we can deduce word meanings:

"ad"	= to, toward	address ("g" in "gress" becomes a "d")
"co, con"	= together	congress (movement together)
"di"	= split	digress (move away from)
"e, ex"	= out of, from	egress (way out, exit)
"in"	= in, into	ingress (way in, entrance)
"pro"	= forward, for	progress (move forward)
"re"	= back	regress (move backward)
"trans"	= across, over	transgress (move across)

So many of the words in English that relate to the intellect, words that make us pause to think and study, come from the Greek. The Roman conquest of Greece and admiration for its culture led to the incorporation of many Greek terms into Latin. So we make a point of studying Greek roots and prefixes as well. For example, the Greek root "pathos" means "feeling" or "suffering", from which come such words as:

"a"	= not	apathy (not caring)
"anti"	= against	antipathy (dislike or hostility)
"em, en"	= into, in	empathy (sharing in another's feeling)
"sym"	= together, with	sympathy (feeling sorrow for another)

In addition, there are other English words based on the same root, such as "pathetic", "pathology", "pathos", and so on.

Consider the common prefixes and cross-connections of the words below:

telecommute	micron	automaton	extrasensory	intercede
telegraph	micrograph	autobiography	extravehicular	intercept
telephone	microphone	automobile	extraterrestrial	interrupt
telescope	microscope	autograph	extraordinary	interdict
television	micromanage	autonomy	extralegal	intervene

or the roots "duc" ("lead"), "fer" ("bear, bring"), "port" ("carry") and "vers" ("turn") as below:

aqueduct	confer	report	converse
conduct	defer	deport	diverse
deduce	refer	transport	reverse
duct	transfer	teleport	adverse
ductile	prefer	airport	perverse
educate	offer	purport	obverse
induce		export	averse
produce		import	inverse
seduce		comport	transverse
viaduct		support	controversy

In the series Building English Vocabulary, a student discovers that from just one Latin or Greek root springs an exponential growth in his vocabulary, sharpened tools to articulate the written or spoken word. A broader knowledge of English leads him to greater ties to the shared cognates of French, Spanish, Italian, and Greek. A stronger grasp of English brings a deeper understanding of the plays of Shakespeare, the novels of Dickens, the essays of Emerson, the poetry of Emily Dickinson, or the oratory of Lincoln and Churchill., who as national leaders, marshaled the English language — the former to invoke peace — the latter to evoke resolve for impending battles, the victories of which in the post bellum of the twentieth century helped thrust English into its role as the lingua franca of the modern world.

Lesson I

AB-, AC-, AMBI-, ANTE-, BENE-, BI-

AB-, ABS-	**AC-, AD-**	**AMBI-**	**ANTE-**	**BENE-**	**BI-**
from, away	to, toward	both	before	good, well	two

> *abduct, abhor, abrasion, abrupt, absorb, accord, adaptable,*
> *adhere, adjacent, adversary, ambidextrous, ambiguous,*
> *ante meridian, anticipate, benediction, benefactor,*
> *bicuspid, bilateral, bilingual, bisect*

Word Definitions

abduct
v. to take away illegally by force or deception; to kidnap
"Paris abducted Helen from Sparta and fled with her to Troy."
abduction (n.)
abducere to lead away: *ab-* away + *ducere* to lead

abhor
v. to regard with loathing; to detest
"She became a vegetarian because she abhorred the slaughter of animals."
abhorrere to shrink away: *ab-* away from + *horrere* to shudder

abrasion
n. the action of, process of, or result of wearing away by friction and rubbing; a scrape
"A slip on the asphalt caused the man to suffer a knee abrasion."
abradere to scrape away: *ab-* away + *radere* to scrape, to shave

abrupt
adj. sudden and unexpected; brief to the point of rudeness; curt
"Feeling suddenly ill, the diner abruptly left the table."
abruptness (n.)
abrumpere to break off, to sever: *ab-* away + *rumpere* to break

absorb
v. to soak up; to assimilate a lesser entity into a larger one; to comprehend
"Distracted by the music, the pupil did not absorb the lesson."
absorbere to swallow, to suck: *ab-* from + *sorbere* to suck in

accord
v. to give or grant someone power or recognition
"Queen Elizabeth accorded a knighthood to Elton John."
n. an official agreement or treaty; a meeting of the minds
"Hostilities ceased when the two sides reached a peace accord."
ad- to + *cor-, cord* heart, mind, spirit

adaptable
adj. able to adjust to new conditions
"Humans are adaptable to all kinds of climates."
adaptability (n.)
adaptare to adjust, to modify: *ad-* to + *aptare* to fit < *aptus* fitting

adhere	v. to stick fast to; to believe in and follow the practices of; to represent truthfully and in detail "Orthodox Jews adhere to strict dietary laws." *adhaerere* to adhere, to cling: *ad-* to + *haerere* to stick
adjacent	adj. next to or adjoining something else; having a common vertex, side, or boundary "Massachusetts is adjacent to five other states." *adjacency (n.)* *adjacere* to lie near: *ad-* to + *jacere* to lie down, to sleep
adversary	n. an opponent or enemy "Barack Obama overcame his adversary, John McCain, to win the presidency in 2008." *adversarial (adj.)* *advertere* to turn toward, to face: *ad-* to + *vertere* to turn
ambidextrous	adj. equally able to use the right and left hands "Grover Cleveland, who was ambidextrous, could write with both hands simultaneously." *ambidexterity (n.)* *ambi-* both + *dexter* right-handed
ambiguous	adj. having more than one meaning, open to different interpretations "The word 'sanction' is ambiguous as it has two opposite meanings." *ambiguus* doubtful, changeable < *ambigere* to hesitate, to doubt: *ambi-* both + *agere* to drive, to act
ante meridian	adj. A.M.; of, relating to, or taking place in the morning "Breakfast is normally an ante meridian meal." *ante-* before + *meridies* noon
anticipate	v. to be aware of in advance; to prepare for; to look forward to "Hannibal was able to anticipate the Romans' moves and thwart them." *anticipare* to take before: *ante-* before + *capere* to take hold, to grasp
benediction	n. the uttering or bestowing of a blessing "The Sunday service closed with the minister's benediction." *benedicere* to bless: *bene* well + *dicere* to say
benefactor	n. a person who gives money or other help to a person or cause "The benefactor gave money to charity anonymously." *bene* good + *facere* to make, to do

bicuspid	**adj.** having two cusps, or points "A crescent moon has a bicuspid form." **n.** a tooth with two cusps, especially a human premolar tooth "The dental hygienist noticed decay on the patient's upper right bicuspid." *bi-* two + *cuspis, cuspidis* sharp point
bilateral	**adj.** having or relating to two sides (usually in mathematics or politics) "Israel and Egypt engaged in direct bilateral negotiations." *bi-* two + *latus* side
bilingual	**adj.** speaking two languages fluently "Most Swiss are at least bilingual, speaking German and French." *bi-* two + *lingua* tongue, language
bisect	**v.** to divide into two parts, usually equal "The Mississippi River roughly bisects the United States." *bisector (n.)* *bi-* two + *secare* to cut

Exercise A

Use the word box at the beginning of the lesson to fill in the blanks below:

1. The Al Qaeda terrorists lured the American journalist away from safety in order to _____ him.

2. Many Democrats _____ the practice of capital punishment.

3. The driver made an _____ evasive maneuver to avoid hitting a squirrel in the middle of the road.

4. When Karen spilled cranberry juice on the kitchen counter, she used a wad of paper towels to _____ the liquid.

5. The cement levee protecting the ocean-front cottage was crumbling after years of _____ from high tides and pounding waves.

6. After decades of fighting over Kashmir, India and Pakistan reached a tentative peace _____.

7. *Spiderman*, starring Toby McGuire as the web-slinger and Willem Dafoe as his _____, the Green Goblin, was so successful that it spawned a blockbuster sequel.

8. Though tempted to keep the paper bag full of money she'd found, Sarah _____ to her ethical principles and tracked down the rightful owner.

9. The SUV was too large for the parking space at Tan-O-Rama, so it ended up occupying half of an _____ space.

10. Since the rain jacket had a removable fleece lining for insulation, it was

_____ for use in any climate or season.

11. Her boss's comments were so _____ that Sarah wasn't sure whether he was praising or blaming her.

12. Some _____ artists draw with one hand and write with another.

13. Seeing the puzzled look on Jessica's face, Nick explained that _____ was a term that meant "before noon".

14. Marco didn't _____ a holiday bonus, because he had begun working for Dynacorp just a few weeks earlier.

15. At the end of the interfaith service, the minister and rabbi pronounced the _____ together.

16. After losing all her baby teeth, Julia noticed that a _____ was beginning to grow next to her molars.

17. The dotted yellow line _____ the highway.

18. Ancient mathematicians found the _____ symmetry of the isosceles triangle so beautiful they included it in the architecture of their greatest buildings.

19. The Museum of Fine Arts in Boston, Massachusetts, recognizes its most generous _____ on a prominent plaque in the lobby.

20. Mr. Banderas grew up in a Spanish-speaking house, but went to an English-speaking school and became _____.

Exercise B
Match the word with the letter of its definition:

1. ____ abduct
2. ____ abhor
3. ____ abrasion
4. ____ abrupt
5. ____ absorb
6. ____ accord
7. ____ adaptable
8. ____ adhere
9. ____ adjacent
10. ____ adversary
11. ____ ambidextrous
12. ____ ambiguous
13. ____ ante meridian
14. ____ anticipate
15. ____ benediction
16. ____ benefactor
17. ____ bicuspid
18. ____ bilateral
19. ____ bilingual
20. ____ bisect

a) to carry off unlawfully
b) to soak up
c) the result of wearing away
d) to detest
e) suddenly change in action or manner
f) an opponent
g) an agreement
h) to stick
i) bordering
j) able to adjust to new situations
k) before noon
l) having more than one interpretation
m) to expect
n) the ability to use left and right hands equally
o) a blessing
p) a double pointed tooth
q) having two sides
r) the ability to speak two languages
s) to divide into two equal parts
t) a person who offers financial support

Exercise C

ACROSS
4 A blessing; an invocation of divine blessing
5 To soak up; to assimilate (a lesser entity) into a larger one
6 Able to use right and left hands equally well
9 To be aware of and prepare for; to look forward to
12 Able to adjust to new conditions
14 To divide into two parts, usually equally
15 Having more than one meaning; open to different interpretations
18 The action of, process of, or result of wearing away by friction
19 To stick fast to; to believe in and follow the practices of

DOWN
1 Relating to or taking place in the morning
2 To take someone away illegally by force or deception
3 To loathe or detest
7 A person who gives money or other help to others
8 Having or relating to two sides
10 Opponent
11 To give or grant someone power or recognition
12 Next to or adjoining something
13 Speaking two languages fluently
16 Having two cusps or points
17 The large muscle in the upper arm with two attachment points
18 Sudden and unexpected; curt; brief to the point of rudeness

Lesson II

CIRCUM-, CO-, CONTRA-, DE-, DIS-, DUO-

| CIRCUM-
around | CO-
together | CONTRA-
against | DE-
down, from | DIS-
apart | DUO-
two |

circulate, circumscribe, circumstantial, collaborate, collision, commiserate, condone, contradict, contraband, contrast, decadence, dedicate, demented, demote, deter, devour, distinct, distortion, distract, duet, duplicate

Word Definitions

circulate v. to move or cause to move around continuously or freely
"Harvey discovered that blood circulates throughout the body."
circulare to move in a circular path < *circulus* circle

circumscribe v. to restrict or limit; to draw a circle around
"A bedridden hospital patient's mobility is circumscribed."
circumscription (n.)
circumscribere to confine; to draw around: *circum-* around + *scribere* to write

circumstantial adj. incidental; dependent on circumstances; suggestive, but not definitive
"No physical proofs linked him to the crime; all the evidence was circumstantial."
circumstare to gather around, to surround: *circum-* around + *stare* to stand

collaborate v. to work together on an activity or project
"I decided to collaborate with him, even though I am the better artist."
collaboration (n.)
collaborare to work with: *co-* together + *laborare* to work

collision n. the act or process of colliding; a crash or conflict
"A collision of views on immigration led to their disagreement."
collide (v.)
collidere to collide: *co-* together + *laedere* to strike

commiserate v. to express sympathy or pity
"The girls commiserated after they were ignored by the same fickle boy."
commiserari to sympathize with: *co-* with + *miserari* to pity, to lament

condone v. to excuse or forgive; to allow to occur; to overlook or give implicit consent to (something)
"The teacher did not condone cheating of any kind."
condonare to make a present of; to forgive: *con-* together + *donare* to give

contraband n. goods that have been imported or exported illegally
"The Border Patrol's task is to seize contraband, such as cocaine."
adj. prohibited from being imported or exported
"The inmate smuggled a carton of contraband cigarettes into the prison."
contra- against + *bannus* proclamation, edict, ban

contradict v. to deny a statement by asserting the opposite
"The laboratory findings contradict the original diagnosis."
contradicere to contradict: *contra-* against + *dicere* to say, to speak

contrast v. to differ strikingly
"Parents' and children's attitudes toward curfews usually contrast."
n. the state of being very different from something else; the degree of difference in colors or tones, especially in art or other visual display
"The bright blue streaks were in striking contrast to the young woman's red hair."
contra- against + *stare* to stand

decadence n. the process or manifestation of moral, physical or cultural decline
"Drunkenness, lewd behavior, and cursing are signs of his decadence."
de- from + *cadere* to fall

dedicate v. to devote solely to a subject, task, or purpose; to address a book or composition
to someone as a sign of respect or affection
"A professional musician dedicates most of his time to practice."
dedicare to devote, to declare: *de-* from + *dicare* to set apart, to devote

demented adj. insane; wild and irrational; suffering from dementia
"The patient believed he was rational, but he was clearly demented."
demens, dementis insane: *de-* from + *mens, mentis* mind, reason

demote v. to revoke a higher rank or senior position
"The disobedient corporal was demoted to the rank of private."
demotion (n.)
de- down + *movere* to move

deter v. to discourage (someone) from doing something by instilling fear of the consequences
"The snowstorm deterred us from attending the party."
deterrere to scare away, to discourage: *de-* away + *terrere* to scare < *terror*

devour v. to consume voraciously or quickly
"After going without food for three days, the rescued man devoured the soup."
devorare to devour, to consume: *de-* down + *vorare* to swallow

distinct adj. dissimilar; different; clear; easily perceived
"To the afficionado, the most distinct pronunciation of Spanish is heard in Valladolid, the ancient seat of the Spanish kings.."
distinctus distinct < *distinguere* to pick out from: *dis-* apart + *stinguere* to prick or stick; to goad

distortion n. the act of twisting (something) out of shape; an untruthful or unfair representation (of something)
"A funhouse mirror causes elongation and distortion of features."
distorquere to twist apart: *dis-* apart + *torquere* turn or twist

distract v. to prevent (someone) from concentrating on something
"I went to a movie to distract me from my sorrow."
distrahere to draw apart: *dis-* apart + *trahere* to draw or drag

duet n. a performance by two singers, instrumentalists, or dancers
"In the opera, the hero and heroine sing a duet."
duo two

duplicate v. to make an exact copy of; to do again unnecessarily
"The boy duplicated his first-inning performance by hitting a second home run."
n. an exact copy
"The painting appeared to be an exact duplicate of the original masterpiece."
adj. exactly like something else; having two corresponding parts
"Make several duplicate copies of this letter, please."
duplicable/duplicative (adj.)
duplicare to double: *duo-* two + *plicare* to fold

Exercise A

Use the word box at the beginning of the lesson to fill in the blanks below.

1. Mike kept searching for the right color to _____ with the dark background of the painting.

2. To help prevent _____ drugs from entering our borders, we need to increase surveillance and security.

3. From all accounts, the accident was preventable, because the lifeguard had clearly _____ the swimming area with a rope.

4. The little girl had the unfortunate habit of _____ her parents' every instruction.

5. During the party, Sam and Paul _____ so they could meet as many new pledges as possible.

6. Mrs. Roberts decided the crumbs on her son's T-shirt provided sufficient _____ evidence of cookie theft.

7. Although they sympathized with their cause, few _____ the radical group's violent acts.

8. The _____ between the car and the pickup truck was so loud we could hear it a block away.

9. The widows _____ over the loss of their husbands during the war.

10. The artist and author _____ to create a children's book with exceptional prose and illustrations.

11. Brad was annoyed when he discovered that his gluttonous friends had _____ all of Jennifer's fabulous chocolate cake.

12. Helen wondered if Jack Nicholson was perhaps _____ himself after watching his stunning portrayals of madmen in *One Flew Over the Cuckoo's Nest* and *The Shining*.

13. Private O'Neill was once a major, but he was _____ after a case of liquor was found in his locker.

14. Supporters of capital punishment claim it _____ crime.

15. The _____ of the kingdom was most obvious at holiday celebrations, when the royals ate and drank to excess.

16. The graduating class _____ the yearbook to Mr. Bragdon, the retiring headmaster.

17. He mumbles when he's talking to himself, but when speaking to others, his words are _____ .

18. Mr. Thomson was embarrassed to learn that his cherished painting was only a _____ of an Old Master.

19. Salvador Dali's _____ of ordinary objects, such as melting watches, is a hallmark of his surrealist paintings.

20. The concert concluded with a _____ performed by the two famous violinists.

21. During the baseball game, the hometown fans tried to _____ the visiting pitcher.

Exercise B

Match the word with the letter of its definition:

1. ____ circulate
2. ____ circumscribe
3. ____ circumstantial
4. ____ collaborate
5. ____ collision
6. ____ commiserate
7. ____ condone
8. ____ contraband
9. ____ contradict
10. ____ contrast
11. ____ decadence
12. ____ dedicate
13. ____ demented
14. ____ demote
15. ____ deter
16. ____ devour
17. ____ distortion
18. ____ distract
19. ____ duet
20. ____ duplicate
21. ____ distinct

a) to say the opposite of
b) striking difference in comparison
c) illegally imported or smuggled goods
d) incidental; dependent on circumstances
e) to move continuously or freely
f) to restrict
g) to excuse or forgive; to overlook
h) to work together on a project
i) to sympathize with the sorrow of another
j) a crash
k) to discourage or prevent from occurring
l) to lower in rank or grade
m) mentally ill; wild and irrational
n) to consume voraciously
o) the process of moral or cultural decline
p) to devote a creative work to a person
q) the action of twisting something out of shape
r) to make an exact copy
s) to draw attention away from
t) a performance by two entertainers
u) different from something else

Exercise C

ACROSS
2 To say the opposite of something or someone
3 To share sorrows with someone else
5 A crash
7 Mentally ill; disturbed
10 A striking difference in comparison
11 To discourage or prevent
12 To consume with great appetite
14 To restrict; to draw a circle around
16 A performance by two artists
17 To lower in rank or grade
18 Of limited significance
19 Illegally imported or smuggled goods

DOWN
1 To make an exact copy
2 To move continuously or freely
4 To address a creative work to a person
6 To work together on a project
8 Different; unique
9 To accept or allow
12 The process of moral or cultural decline
13 A twisting or misrepresentation
15 To draw attention away

Lesson III
EQUI-, EX-, EXTRA-, IN-, IL-, INTER-, INTRA-

EQUI-	EX-	EXTRA-	IN-	IL-, IM-, IN-	INTER-	INTRA-
equal	out	beyond	in, on	not, against	among	within

> *equity, equivalent, emigrate, eradicate, evoke,
> extrovert, illuminate, implicate, inclusive, inscription,
> illegible, illiterate, incessant, irrelevant, interjection,
> interlude, intersect, intervene, intravenous, introvert*

Word Definitions

equity
n. fairness and impartiality; the value of shares issued by a company; value of a property or asset minus any debts against it
"The judge was known for his equity in commercial disputes."
aequitas justice, impartiality < *equus* equal

equivalent
adj. equal or nearly equal in value, amount, function, or meaning
"100 degrees Celsius and 212 degrees Fahrenheit are equivalent."
equivalence (n.)
aequivalere to be of equal worth or power: *aequi-* equal + *valere* to be strong, to prevail

emigrate
v. to leave one's native country to reside in another
"The Irish emigrated from their homeland to escape the potato famine."
emigration (n.), emigrant (n.)
emigrare to emigrate: *ex-* out + *migrare* to move

eradicate
v. to remove or destroy completely
"Smallpox was eradicated in the U.S. several decades ago."
eradication (n.)
eradicare to tear up by the roots: *ex-* out + *radicare* to take root

evoke
v. to recall to the conscious mind; to bring out
"A small cake dipped in tea evoked a torrent of memory in Proust."
evocation (n.)
evocare to call forth: *ex-* out of + *vocare* to call

extrovert
n. an outgoing, socially confident person
"Cheerleaders typically are extroverts."
extroversion (n.), extroverted (adj.)
extra- outside + *vertere* to turn

illuminate	**v.** to light up "Large windows illuminated the upper floors, while the finished basement had recessed lighting." *illumination (n.)* *illuminare* to illuminate: *il-* in (expressing intensity) + *luminare* to light up
implicate	**v.** to show to be involved in a crime or mishap; to incriminate "A faulty tile was implicated in the failure of the space shuttle." *implication (n.)* *implicare* to involve, to entangle: *im-* in + *plicare* to fold
inclusive	**adj.** including the limits specified; containing as part of the whole "The school aims to be inclusive, admitting Muslims, Jews, and Christians." *includere* to include; to imprison: *in-* into + *claudere* to enclose
inscription	**n.** words written, as on a monument or in a book "The famous inscription on the Rosetta Stone is in three languages." *Inscribere* to inscribe or record: *in-* into + *scribere* to write
illegible	**adj.** not clear enough to be read "'You must print the information on the form; your handwriting is illegible." *illegibility (n.)* *il-* not + *legere* to read
illiterate	**adj.** unable to read or write "Uniformly illiterate, pharaohs relied on scribes to read and write." *illiteracy (n.)* *il-* not + *littera* letter; books
incessant	**adj.** continuing without pause or interruption (often unpleasantly) "A beehive is an incessant buzz of activity." *in-* not + *cessare* to cease
irrelevant	**adj.** not closely connected to (something); not mattering; unimportant "Since all work was done indoors, the weather was irrelevant." *irrelevance (n.)* *ir-* not + *relevare* to raise up; to elevate
interjection	**n.** a remark inserted when someone else is speaking; an exclamation "'Ach!' is an interjection in both Scottish and German." *interject (v.)* *interjacere* to interpose or insert: *inter-* between + *jacere* to throw
interlude	**n.** a dissimilar event or period between two others; an intermission "The Great Depression occurred during the interlude between world wars." *interludium* interlude, episode: *inter-* between + *ludus* play
intersect	**v.** to divide across or through; to cross; to meet at a point "The road near my house intersects a state highway." *intersection (n.)* *intersecare* to cut apart, to divide: *inter-* between + *secare* to cut

intervene	**v.** to come between; to occur as an unplanned circumstance
	"The policeman intervened to end the fistfight."
	intervention (n.)
	intervenire to come between: *inter-* between + *venire* to come
intravenous	**adj.** within or into a vein or veins
	"Medicines administered by needle are intravenous."
	intra- within + *vena* vein
introvert	**n.** a shy, reticent person (opposite of extrovert)
	"An introvert, he greatly preferred reading at home to going out."
	introversion (n.), introverted (adj.)
	intro- to the inside + *vertere* to turn

Exercise A

Use the word box at the beginning of the lesson to fill in the blanks below:

1. When two formulas express the same value, they are _____.

2. Lo-Han's parents _____ from China while in their teens.

3. Although Yellow Fever has been _____ in the United States, it still exists in countries unable to properly vaccinate against it.

4. Carrot Top could not _____ laughter from an audience, even if he were to run around in clown shoes with his pants on fire.

5. The value of a company's _____ usually exceeds the value of the bonds it issues.

6. You would think that all professional actors are _____ by nature, but in fact many of them are quite reserved off camera.

7. Adding a floodlight will better _____ the front door and steps.

8. The witness could not testify without _____ herself in the crime.

9. The club was very _____; anyone interested in coin collecting could join.

10. The book is very valuable because an _____ inside the front cover shows it was a gift from the author to his mistress.

11. Doctors are required to sign so many documents each day that their signatures rapidly become _____ strings of loops and lines.

12. He claims that gender is _____ in the workplace, but I notice that he only promotes men to the top jobs, even when there are qualified women candidates.

13. Creating stable and well-balanced economies in third-world countries is a momentous task, because in many nations most workers are _____ and therefore ill-equipped to handle jobs that require reading or writing.

14. The _____ call of the raven in Edgar Allen Poe's poem drives the narrator to madness.

15. New York City is far easier to navigate than Boston, because the streets of New York _____ at right angles, while roads in Boston cross at arbitrary angles.

16. During the intermission, the Boston Pops played a brief _____.

17. _____ drugs affect the patient more rapidly than those taken orally because they enter the bloodstream immediately.

18. Although he exudes confidence and charm on camera, Toby McGuire describes himself as an _____.

19. The crossing guard tried to _____ in the fight, but got only a bloody nose for his efforts.

20. Stephen exclaimed "Holy cow!" when he saw the shooting star, but his _____ failed to stop the argument between his parents.

Exercise B

Match the word with the letter of its definition:

1. ____ equity
2. ____ equivalent
3. ____ emigrate
4. ____ eradicate
5. ____ evoke
6. ____ extrovert
7. ____ illuminate
8. ____ implicate
9. ____ inclusive
10. ____ inscription
11. ____ illegible
12. ____ illiterate
13. ____ incessant
14. ____ irrelevant
15. ____ interjection
16. ____ interlude
17. ____ intersect
18. ____ intervene
19. ____ intravenous
20. ____ introvert

a) to get rid of entirely
b) equal in all respects
c) to call forth
d) to leave one's country for another
e) an outgoing person
f) value of property after debts
g) to show to be involved in a crime
h) to light up; to shed light on
i) including the limits specified
j) words written on a monument
k) the time between two events
l) to cut across or through
m) difficult or impossible to read
n) continuing without interruption
o) unable to read or write
p) off the subject
q) an exclamation
r) a shy person
s) to come between
t) into vein(s)

Exercise C

ACROSS
1 To show to be involved in a crime
7 To bring or recall to the conscious mind
8 Not closely connected or important to the matter at hand
9 To remove or destroy completely
12 A sudden, short utterance
14 Within or into a vein or veins
15 To come between; to occur as an unplanned circumstance
16 Equal in value, amount, function, or meaning
17 Continuing without pause interruption (especially something unpleasant)

DOWN
1 To divide something by passing across it
2 Not clear enough to be read
3 An intervening period of time; something occurring or done during an interval
4 An outgoing person, socially confident, overtly expressive
5 To leave one's own country in order to settle permanently in another
6 Quality of being fair and impartial; value of shares in a company or mortgaged property
8 Unable to read or write
10 To light up
11 Including the limits specified; containing as part of a whole
12 Words written, as on a monument or in a book
13 A shy, reticent, or unexpressive person

Lesson IV

MAGNUS-, MAL-, MULTI-, OB-, OMNI-, PER-, POST-, PRE-

MAGNUS-	***MAL-***	***MULTI-***	***OB-***	***OMNI-***	***PER-***	***POST-***	***PRE-***
big	**bad**	**many**	**against, toward**	**all**	**through**	**After**	**before**

> *magnificent, magnitude, major, majority, malicious,*
> *multilateral, multitude, obligation, obliterate, obsess,*
> *omnivorous, persevere, perspective, posterity,*
> *postpone, postscript, preclude, prediction, presume*

Word Definitions

magnificent   **adj.** very beautiful, elaborate, or impressive
"The Great Pyramid of Gaza is a magnificent tribute to King Khufu."
magnificare to prize, to praise: *magnus* great + *facere* to make

magnitude   **n.** size, extent, or importance
"Matt realized the magnitude of his ignorance after he failed the test."
magnitudo size, bulk, greatness < *magnus* great

major   **adj.** important, serious, or significant; great or large (in size)
"George Soros was a major contributor to Obama's presidential campaign."
n. a military or police rank; a student's principal course of study
"After taking an introductory course, she decided to major in electrical engineering."
major < *magnus* great

majority   **n.** more than half; most
"A presidential candidate in the United States must win a majority of votes in the Electoral College – but not a majority of the popular vote – to be elected."
magnus great

malicious   **adj.** intending harm or intended to do harm
"Sticking pins in a voodoo doll shows malicious intent."
malice (n.)
malignus tending to evil < *malus* bad

multilateral   **adj.** agreed upon or done by three or more political parties or nations
"Japan, the United States, Russia, and China have joined North and South Korea in multilateral talks over the northern state's nuclear weapons program."
multi- many + *latus* side

multitude	**n.** a large number of people or things; the mass of ordinary people "A multitude of locusts blackened the sky, then alit in the cornfields." *multitudo* great number, crowd or mob < *multus* many
obligation	**n.** an act or course of action to which a person is legally or morally bound "It once was an obligation for all men to serve in the military." *oblige (v.)* *obligare* to bind, to oblige: *ob-* toward (expressing intensity) + *ligare* to bind
obliterate	**v.** to destroy utterly; to wipe out; to erase "After she broke his heart, he tried to obliterate all reminders of her." *obliteration (n.)* *obliterare* to cause to be forgotten, to strike out: *ob-* against + *littera* letter, something written
obsess	**v.** to be continually preoccupied with, or intensely focused on (something or someone) "Ahab was so obsessed with capturing Moby Dick that he endangered the lives of his crew." *obsession (n.)* *obsidere* to besiege or occupy: *ob-* toward (expressing intensity) + *sidere* to settle (on something)
omnivorous	**adj.** eating food of both plant and animal origin "Humans are omnivorous, which allows them to adapt to a wide variety of climates." *omnivore (n.)* *omni-* all + *vorare* to eat
perforate	**v.** to pierce and make a hole or holes in "Band-Aids are perforated with tiny holes to allow air flow." *perforation (adj.)* *perforare* to pierce through: *per-* completely + *forare* to pierce
persevere	**v.** to continue a course of action despite difficulty or low odds of success "Because the tortoise persevered, he beat the hare." *perseverance (n.)* *perseverare* to persist < *perseverus* very strict: *per-* thoroughly + *severus* severe
perspective	**n.** (1) an artistic technique for representing distance and three-dimensional objects on a flat surface; a view or prospect "The use of perspective in Renaissance drawing gave an appearance of depth and dimension." **n.** (2) a point of view "The war seems very different when analyzing it from Iraq's perspective." *perspicere* to examine closely: *per-* thoroughly + *specere* to look
posterity	**n.** future generations; all the descendants of one person "Public libraries were Franklin's gift to posterity." *posterus* coming after; descendants < *post* after, behind

postpone v. to put off until later (something scheduled or due)
"The cross-examination was postponed after the witness fell ill."
postponere to set aside: *post* after + *ponere* to place

postscript n. an additional remark at the end of a letter; a brief sequel
"A postscript added after the signature at the bottom of a letter is abbreviated 'P.S.'"
postscribere to write under: *post* after + *scribere* to write

preclude v. to prevent (someone from doing something); to prevent (something) from happening
"Her infirmities preclude her from living a normal life."
praecludere to close or block: *prae-* before + *claudere* to shut

prediction n. a forecast
"The Oracle of Delphi issued strange predictions, which were interpreted and written down by priests."
predict (v.)
praedicere to say beforehand: *prae-* before + *dicere* to say

presume v. to suppose (something) is true or take it for granted; to venture (to do something)
"Dewey was the presumed victor, but in the end Truman won."
presumptuous (adj.), presumption (n.)
praesumere to anticipate, to take for granted: *prae-* before + *sumere* to take

Exercise A
Use the word box at the beginning of the lesson to fill in the blanks below:

1. The view outside Rachel's apartment window, of the setting sun casting a purple glow on the snowy mountains, was _____.

2. The _____ agreement among the western European nations will promote trade.

3. Harold did not know whether to declare physics or chemistry as his _____ at MIT.

4. He was clearly a _____ person, always hoping that others would be thwarted or humiliated.

5. The ferocity of the tropical storm caught the deep sea fishing vessel by surprise; the crew was not expecting a tempest of such _____.

6. In a democratic nation, the _____ vote usually determines who will be elected.

7. After scoring the winning goal for Spain in the World Cup, Cristiano Ronaldo smiled at the _____ of ecstatic fans before collapsing from exhaustion.

8. Fish and Game divers and volunteers worked to _____ milfoil, an invasive weed that crowds out native plants and harms fish populations, from the lake.

9. Derek spent his vacation in Spain _____ over his upcoming exams, instead of enjoying the attractions and museums.

10. He didn't want to serve on the budget committee, but felt it was an _____ he couldn't sidestep.

11. A marathon is a test not only of an athlete's physical condition, but also his or her willingness to _____ through pain and exhaustion.

12. The hole punch _____ the construction paper so it could be put in the binder.

13. From Steve's _____, the ball appeared to land in bounds, but the line judge declared it out.

14. Though Susan simply meant that John was not a vegetarian, everyone found it funny that she called him _____, because he seemed to eat everything in sight.

15. Although it had begun to drizzle, the fans had already arrived, so the referee was reluctant to _____ the game.

16. Mike's _____ that *Chicago* would not win anything at the Academy Awards appeared foolish when the movie won seven Oscars, including "Best Picture."

17. Starring in *The Lord of the Rings* trilogy _____ actor Elijah Wood from accepting any other roles for the entire, three-year production period.

18. With no physical description or photo to go by, Hank could only _____ that the woman sitting alone at a table was his blind date, Elizabeth.

19. Indiana Jones was able to decipher the cryptic letter when he realized that the seemingly innocuous _____, "P.S. Don't forget to feed the cat," was actually a coded message referring to the Nazis on his trail.

20. We need to pay down the national debt so that it is manageable for _____ .

Exercise B

Match the word with the letter of its definition:

1. ____ magnificent
2. ____ magnitude
3. ____ major
4. ____ majority
5. ____ malicious
6. ____ multilateral
7. ____ multitude
8. ____ obligation
9. ____ obliterate
10. ____ obsess
11. ____ omnivorous
12. ____ perforate
13. ____ persevere
14. ____ perspective
15. ____ posterity
16. ____ postpone
17. ____ post script
18. ____ preclude
19. ____ prediction
20. ____ presume

a) a great throng of people or things
b) a rank in the army
c) involving three or more parties
d) more than half of a group
e) spectacular; exceptional
f) scope or importance
g) intending to do harm
h) a duty
i) to utterly destroy
j) to think about constantly
k) to remain devoted to a difficult task
l) to make a hole in; to pierce
m) a point of view
n) feeding on both plants and animals
o) to put off to a later time
p) future generations
q) to make an assumption
r) a claim about future events
s) to make impossible; to prevent
t) an added note at the end of a letter

Exercise C

ACROSS
3 Feeding on plants and animal food; taking in or using whatever is available
4 To cause or arrange for something to take place later than first scheduled
6 To destroy utterly; to wipe out, erase
8 To suppose that something is the case based on probability; to take for granted
9 A technique of representing three-dimensional objects on a two-dimensional surface
10 A forecast
12 Very beautiful, elaborate or impressive
13 Important, serious or significant
14 An act or course of action to which a person is legally or morally bound
15 Future generations of people
16 Intending to do harm
17 A large number of people or things; the mass of ordinary people

DOWN
1 An additional remark at the end of a letter, after the signature
2 To prevent someone from doing something; to prevent something from happening
5 To continue in a course of action in spite of difficulty or with little or no indication of success
6 To focus exclusively on something
7 Agreed upon or participated in by three or more parties
10 To pierce and make a hole or holes in
11 Size, extent or importance
12 More than half; most

Lesson V

PRIM-, PRO-, RE-, RETRO-, SE-, SUB-, SUPER-, TRANS-, UNI-

PRIM-, first	***PRO-*** forward, in front of	***RE-*** back, again	***RETRO-*** back, backwards
SE- apart, aside, away	***SUB-*** under	***SUPER-*** above, over	***TRANS-*** across, beyond
UNI- one			

> *primary, primate, procession, proceed, profit,*
> *provoke, recite, recline, reiterate, retrospect,*
> *seclude, secure, subscribe, suffocate, suggest,*
> *supervise, translucent, transparent, unanimous, unity*

Word Definitions

primary **adj.** of chief importance, principal; earliest in time or order; an election within a party to determine its candidates for the general election (U.S.)
"His job was the family's primary means of support."
primarius of the first rank; distinguished < *primus* first

primate **n.** a mammal of the order including humans, monkeys and gorillas; an archbishop or bishop who is more important than others in a region
"Unlike our close primate relatives, we humans walk upright."
primas first, best < *primus* first

procession/proceed **n.** a number of people or vehicles moving forward in an orderly fashion; a parade; **v.** go forward or onward, continue without interuption
"The procession of job seekers continued throughout the day."
"On an icy road, one should proceed with caution."
procedere advance: *pro-* forward + *cedere* to go

profit **v.** to benefit from
"The car salesman profited from the resale of the used truck."
n. a financial gain; proceeds; an advantage or benefit;
"When he retired, he lived off the profit from his investments."
profectus profit, progress < *proficere* to advance; to progress: *pro-* ahead + *facere* to make

provoke **v.** to cause something to happen; to annoy
"Exposure to poison oak may provoke a rash."
provocative (adj.), *provocation* (n.)
provocare to challenge: *pro-* forth + *vocare* to call

30

recite   **v.** to repeat aloud from memory; to state in order
"Children are often required to recite poems in school."
recitation (n.)
recitare to read out: *re-* back, again + *citare* to cite, to quote

recline   **v.** to lean against or lie back in a relaxed manner
"He reclined on the bench, smoking and studying her insolently."
reclining (adj.)
reclinare to bend back: *re-* back + *clinare* to bend

reiterate   **v.** to say something again; to restate
"I said it before and I'll say it again: No new taxes!"
reiteration (n.)
reiterare to go over again: *re-* (expressing repetition) + *iterare* to revise or renew

retrospect **n.** a survey or review of a past course of events
"At the time, it seemed like a good idea. In retrospect, I see that it wasn't."
retrospective (adj.)
retro- backward + *prospectus* view

seclude   **v.** to shut someone away from other people
"J. D. Salinger refused interview requests and lived a secluded life."
seclusion (n.)
secludere shut off or apart: *se-* apart + *claudere* to shut

secure   **v.** to obtain; to fasten; to protect against threats
"The Harvard Law grad secured a job as a Supreme Court clerk."
adj. fixed or fastened so as not to give way, become loose, or be lost; protected against attack; free from fear or anxiety; safe
"The wounded soldier had to be moved to a secure area before he could be given medical attention."
security (n.)
securus safe, untroubled: *se-* apart + *cura* care, concern

subscribe   **v.** to arrange to receive something (such as a periodical); to agree with
"I don't subscribe to the Republican economic agenda."
subscription (n.)
subscribere to subscribe, to underwrite: *sub-* under + *scribere* to write

suffocate   **v.** to be unable to breathe; to stop someone from breathing; to die from lack of air
"Putting dirt or sand on a campfire will suffocate the flames."
suffocation (n.)
suffocare to stifle: *sub-* below + *fauces* throat

suggest   **v.** to put forward for consideration; to hint at
"His muddy boots suggested it was raining outside."
suggestion (n.), suggestive (adj.)
suggerere to suggest, to prompt: *sub-* from below + *gerere* to carry, to manage

supervise　　　v. to oversee and direct the execution of a task or activity
"A foreman supervises the workers and is responsible for quality."
supervision (n.), supervisor (n.)
super- over + *videre* to see

translucent　　adj. allowing some light to pass through; semi-transparent
"Stained glass is translucent, while clear glass is transparent."
translucence (n.)
translucere: to shine through: *trans-* across (through) + *lucere* to shine

transparent　　adj. (of a substance) allowing light to pass through so that objects behind can be distinctly seen; (of someone) easy to see through
"His true motives were transparent to everyone but his adoring wife."
transparency (n.)
transparere to show through: *trans-* across (through) + *parere* to show

unanimous　　adj. fully in agreement; universally in accord
"The court's decision was unanimous, surprising those who had expected Justice Scalia to dissent."
unanimity (n.)
unanimus acting in accord: *uni-* one, single + *animus* mind, spirit

unity　　　　n. the state of being united; forming a complex whole
"After the terrorist attacks of Sept. 11, 2001, American politicians displayed a rare unity in the face of the nation's enemies."
unitas oneness < *unus* one

Exercise A

Use the word box at the beginning of the lesson to fill in the blanks below:

1. Every four years, New Hampshire hosts the nation's first presidential _____, but prospective candidates start visiting the state a year earlier to see if they can drum up support.

2. When Suzy the chimp escaped the zoo, it took the animal control officer weeks to locate the resourceful _____, who slept in trees and scavenged from garbage cans.

3. After the plane landed, the airline steward announced that we should _____ to the baggage claim.

4. Oftentimes during a funeral, a black hearse will lead a _____ of cars, which by law no vehicle other than an emergency vehicle may interrupt.

5. All during school, Mike _____ Susan by grabbing her ponytail and yanking it.

6. Since its founding, the company has increased its _____ by 10% annually.

7. To qualify for the summer trip around the country, each student had to memorize and _____ the Gettysburg Address.

8. After the Red Sox committed three errors in the ninth inning to lose the game, the manager _____ the importance of defense.

9. In _____, we might have been able to move in earlier, if we had not taken our vacation before I transferred to the new job.

10. Chairs that _____ are far more comfortable than ones that do not.

11. Betsey sought out a bench in a _____ spot where she could be alone with her thoughts.

12. The Secret Service tried to find a _____ location for the president on Martha's Vineyard, in case of a terrorist attack during his summer vacation.

13. Peter _____ the project, while Amanda and Mike implemented it.

14. Members of the acting class _____ numerous possibilities for the school musical before agreeing on *Oklahoma!*

15. She felt as if she would _____ if she didn't escape from the vile fumes as quickly as possible.

16. I read the same newspaper all of the time, but I _____ to a different magazine each year.

17. The outcome was _____; the entire class voted to go on a whale watch at the end of the year.

18. The new _____ curtains made the room appear lighter and brighter.

19. Our team's _____ helped us win the championship; the other team had some better players, but they were *prima donnas*.

20. Glass greenhouses remain _____ for decades, while clear plastics, although more durable, can become scratched and cloudy quickly.

Exercise B
Match the word with the letter of its definition:

1. ____ primary
2. ____ primate
3. ____ proceed
4. ____ procession
5. ____ profit
6. ____ provoke
7. ____ recite
8. ____ recline
9. ____ reiterate
10. ____ retrospect
11. ____ seclude
12. ____ secure
13. ____ supervise
14. ____ subscribe
15. ____ suffocate
16. ____ suggest
17. ____ translucent
18. ____ transparent
19. ____ unanimous
20. ____ unity

a) humans, gorillas, and monkeys
b) a parade
c) to benefit financially
d) first in rank or importance
e) to begin a course of action
f) to deliberately annoy or anger
g) to say again
h) a review of past events
i) to repeat by memory
j) to lean back or lie down
k) to protect against threats
l) to put forward for consideration
m) to oversee
n) to remove from social interaction; to isolate
o) make unable to breathe
p) to arrange to receive periodically
q) oneness
r) allowing light to pass through partially
s) see-through
t) completely in agreement

Exercise C

ACROSS

3. To be unable to breathe or to die from lack of air
5. To benefit from
6. To observe and direct the execution of a task
7. A survey or review of the past course of events
9. The first among a group of bishops or archbishops
10. To repeat aloud from memory before an audience
12. To keep away from other people
14. Of chief importance or principal; an election within a party to select its candidates
16. To affix or fasten; to protect against threats
17. To begin a course of action; to move forward
18. Allowing light to pass through so that objects may be seen distinctly; having thoughts or feelings that are easily perceived
19. To lean or lie back in a relaxed position
20. Fully in agreement; universally in accord

DOWN

1. To arrange to receive something; to agree with a position or point of view
2. The state of being united, forming a complex whole
4. To annoy or anger deliberately
8. Allowing light to pass though partially
11. To put forward for consideration; to hint at
13. A number or people moving forward in an orderly fashion
15. To say something again

Quiz 1

> *magnificent, postpone, provoke, obliterate, evoke,
> retrospect, bilingual, anticipated, emigrate, demote,
> unity, eradicate, condone, abhor, secluded, multitude,
> interjection, demote, irrelevant, intersection, unity*

1. She _____ her upcoming wedding with a mixture of excitement and dread.

2. In _____, the coach should have called a time out, but he hoped the players would rally and remember how to run an effective defense.

3. Even though they do not _____ violence, the police may, at times, be forced to resort to violent behavior themselves.

4. "And above all things, have fervent charity among yourselves: for charity shall cover the _____ of sins." Peter 4:8

5. He tried to _____ a reaction by clowning around, but the other kids ignored him.

6. After Rome conquered Egypt, the authorities tried to _____ all hieroglyphs in order to _____ all remnants of the Egyptians' culture and language.

7. Most coaches try to promote _____ by emphasizing teamwork and not comparing the abilities of individual players.

8. The counselors _____ the trip to the water park because of _____ thunderstorms.

9. Some teams in the NBA are so atrocious that the commissioner may _____ them to a developmental league.

10. In poetry, authors use symbolism and metaphors to _____ emotion in the reader.

11. Red Sox fans are known to _____ the Yankees, and vice-versa.

12. The mansion was _____, but the family chose not to buy the home because it was too _____ and isolated.

13. After the Polish family _____ to the United States, the children quickly became _____ because they spoke English in school all day long.

14. The rude student continuously made unnecessary _____ and _____ remarks.

15. The _____ of Chestnut and Main streets can be very dangerous because many drivers speed through the crosswalk without stopping.

36

Lesson VI

AC-, AG-, AGRI-, ALI-, ALT-, ALTI-, AMOR-,
AMBUL-, ANIM-, ANNUS, APER-, APT-

| **AC-, ACR-** | **AG-, ACT-** | **AGRI-, AGRARI-** | **ALI-** | **ALT-** |
| sharp | drive, move | field | another | other |

| **ALTI-** | **AMOR-** | **AMBUL-** | **ANIM-** |
| high | love | walk | mind, soul, will |

| | **ANNUS** | **APER-** | **APT-** |
| | year | open | fit |

> *acrid, acute, agility, agitate, agriculture, alias, alien, alienate, alter, altitude, amateur, amiable, ambulatory, animate, animosity, annual, annuity, aperture, aptitude, inept*

Word Definitions

acrid **adj.** unpleasantly bitter or pungent; biting or bitter (remarks)
"The acrid smoke made our eyes water and our throats burn."
acridity (n.)
acer, acri- sharp, pungent

acute **adj.** perceptive, finely honed; (of a situation) dire, severe; (of a disease) of sudden onset and short duration
"Migratory birds need an acute sense of direction."
acuere to sharpen < *acus* needle

agility **n.** the state or quality of being nimble
"An Olympic gymnast's routines require great agility."
agile (adj.)
agere to drive, to urge

agitate **v.** to upset (someone) or make them nervous; to arouse public opinion for a cause; to shake vigorously
"Although he knew the music annoyed Matt, Steve made it louder simply to agitate him."
agitare to set in motion

agriculture **n.** the science or practice of farming
"Agriculture in the U.S. has shifted from small family farms to large, corporate agribusinesses."
ager field + *cultura* growing, cultivation

alias n. a false or assumed identity; an alternative name or label
"William Bonney was better known by his alias, Billy the Kid."
alius other, another, different

alien adj. belonging to a foreign country; unfamiliar and distasteful
"He found his surroundings alien when he first emigrated."
n. a foreigner; a being from another world
"About 20 percent of Americans believe space aliens exist and visit our planet."
alius other, another, different

alienate v. to cause to feel isolated; to estrange
"His nasty gossip alienated his friend and ended their relationship."
alienare to estrange or lose possession < *alias* other, different

alter v. to change in character, appearance, or composition; to adjust clothing for a better fit; to spay a domestic animal
"Global warming threatens to alter the climate for the worse."
alter other

altitude n. the height of an object or point in relation to sea level or ground level
"As altitude climbs from sea level to mountaintop, the air thins."
altus high

amateur n. a person who does an activity for love, not money; a person considered inept at a particular activity
"The tennis pro handily defeated most amateurs, even the most devoted players."
adj. non-professional; inept, unskillful
"The amateur skateboarder loved to learn new tricks."
amare to love

amiable adj. friendly and pleasant in manner
"I warmed to my new acquaintance quickly for he was an amiable fellow."
amicus friend, loved one

ambulatory adj. walking or able to walk; movable, mobile
"After the motorcycle accident, she was no longer ambulatory without a wheelchair."
ambulare to walk

animate v. to give life or vigor to; to give the appearance of movement
"Dr. Frankenstein animated a dead body, creating a semi-human monster."
adj. alive or having life
"He manipulated the marionettes so skillfully they seemed animate."
animation (n.)
animare to give to life, to revive < *animus* spirit, mind, life

animosity n. strong hostility
"Dogs display animosity by baring their teeth and growling."
animositas boldness, vehemence, wrath < *animus* spirit, mind, life

annual	**adj.** occurring once every year; calculated over or covering a year; (of a plant) dying after one season (contrast with perennial) "He stopped holding the annual company Christmas party after his wife died." **n.** a book or magazine of a series published once a year; an annual plant "She bought some annuals at the garden store." *annus* year
annuity	**n.** a fixed sum of money paid to someone each year, typically for the rest of their lives; an investment that yields such an income "A sizable annuity allowed him to travel the world after he retired." *annus* year
aperture	**n.** an opening, hole, or gap "A camera's aperture is the lens opening that allows light to enter." *aperire* to open, to reveal
aptitude	**n.** a natural ability or propensity "Unlike her brother, the girl showed a strong aptitude for mathematics." *aptus* fitted < *apere* to fasten, to join
inept	**adj.** incompetent; awkward or clumsy "The new kid proved inept as a catcher." *ineptitude (n.)* *ineptus:* in- not + *aptus* fitted < *apere* to fasten, to join

Exercise A

Use the word box at the beginning of the lesson to fill in the blanks below:

1. Her _____ comments made him redden with embarrassment and anger.

2. Superman's _____ is Clark Kent.

3. Nastia Liukin's _____, strength, and grace won her the gold medal in gymnastics in the 2008 Olympics.

4. The pilot said the airplane's cruising _____ was 30,000 feet.

5. Nick had an _____ sense of smell: He could tell from a block away when Grandma Lachey was making his favorite strawberry-rhubarb pie.

6. We did not mean to _____ the ants, but when we accidentally stepped on the anthill, they began to swarm around the opening.

7. Because the English teacher was known for giving extra assignments for misbehavior or a poor attitude, her students tried hard not to _____ her.

8. When her metabolism began to slow down, Suzanne Somers had to _____ her diet to maintain her svelte physique.

9. Foreigners who enter the United States without legal permission are called illegal _____.

10. _____ accounts for a dwindling share of the U.S. economy, although small organic farms are on the rise.

11. Theodora's _____ income tripled in one year as a result of increased sales.

12. The first construction crew was so _____ that the entire addition had to be torn down and rebuilt by a more competent contractor.

13. When they shared the stage at the Video Music Awards, one could sense the _____ between the feuding divas.

14. The museum requested that the tour guides _____ their presentations to attract more visitors.

15. Miriam was a complete _____ and never should have been hired for the highly skilled position.

16. Mozart had an innate _____ for music: He displayed dazzling talent at an extraordinarily young age.

17. By adjusting the size of the camera _____, a photographer can control the amount of light that enters the lens when she releases the shutter.

18. Since my $10,000 _____ has a yield of 6 percent, I get a check for $600 each year.

19. His _____ disposition and charisma contributed to Tony Blair's success in establishing good relationships with other politicians.

20. The late Christopher Reeve, the star of the movie *Superman*, who became paralyzed from the neck down, vowed to become fully _____ again.

Exercise B
Match the word with the letter of its definition:

1. ____ acrid
2. ____ acute
3. ____ agility
4. ____ agitate
5. ____ agriculture
6. ____ alias
7. ____ alien
8. ____ alienate
9. ____ alter
10. ____ altitude
11. ____ amateur
12. ____ amiable
13. ____ ambulatory
14. ____ animate
15. ____ animosity
16. ____ annual
17. ____ annuity
18. ____ aperture
19. ____ aptitude
20. ____ inept

a) yearly
b) nimbleness
c) foreign
d) to change
e) height from the ground or sea level
f) to bring to life; to inspire
g) pungent and bitter
h) farming
i) incompetent
j) a strong hostility
k) able to walk; mobile
l) very perceptive
m) an opening
n) to disturb
o) a false label or name
p) to estrange
q) a non-professional
r) a yearly payment of money
s) a natural ability
t) friendly

Exercise C

ACROSS
1. A natural ability or propensity
3. To change in character, appearance, or composition
4. To give life or vigor to; to give the appearance of movement
6. A false or assumed identity
9. Strong hostility
10. Occurring once every year
12. The state or quality of being nimble
13. Friendly and pleasant in manner
14. A person who does an activity for love, not money
15. The science or practice of farming

DOWN
1. Perceptive, finely honed; dire, severe
2. Incompetent; awkward or clumsy
4. To upset someone or make them nervous
5. Belonging to a foreign country
7. A fixed sum of money paid to someone each year
8. Walking or able to walk; movable, mobile
10. To isolate or estrange something or someone
11. An opening, hole, or gap
12. The height of an object in relation to sea level
13. Unpleasantly bitter or pungent

Lesson VII

ARM-, ART-, AUD-, AVUNCULUS, BATTU-, BEATUS,
BELLI, BIB-, BREVE, CAD-, CALCITR-, CAND-,
CANT-, CAP-

ARM- weapon	*ART-* skill, craft	*AUD-* to hear	*AVUNCULUS* uncle	
BATTU- beat	*BEATUS* blessed	*BELLI* war	*BIB-* to drink	*BREVE* brevity
CAD-, CAS fall	*CALCITR-* to kick, resist	*CAND-* white, glow	*CANT-* to sing	*CAP-, CIP-* to take

> *army, artifact, artificial, audible, audience, auditorium, avuncular, battery, beatitude, rebellious, imbibe, abbreviation, brevity, casualty, recalcitrant, candid, candidate, incantation, capture, participate*

Word Definitions

army
n. an organized military force; a large number of similar people or things
"The highly unpopular politician faced an army of critics."
armare to arm

artifact
n. an object made by a human being
"Archaeological sites in Egypt yielded artifacts showing a high degree of skill among ancient artisans."
ars, artis craft, art + *factum* something made

artificial
adj. not natural; man-made; untruthful
"Artificial flowers may deceive initially, but not on closer inspection."
artificium art, craft, technology: *ars, artis* art + *facere* to make

audible
adj. able to be heard
"The music was audible from across the lawn."
audire to hear

audience
n. the assembled spectators or listeners at an event; the readership of a book, magazine, or newspaper; a formal interview with a person in authority
"The Pope rarely grants an audience to ordinary churchgoers."
audire to hear

auditorium
n. the part of a theater or hall in which an audience sits
"The crowd milled about the auditorium while the musicians tuned up."

audire to hear

avuncular   **adj.** like an uncle in being kind and friendly toward a younger or less experienced person
"Santa Claus is portrayed as a rosy-cheeked, avuncular figure."
avunculus maternal uncle

battery   **n.** a container consisting of one or more cells in which chemical energy is converted into electricity to be used as a source of power; any large group of things; striking of one person by another; two or more pieces of artillery
"He was charged with assault and battery after he smashed a cream pie into the newspaper owner's face."
battuere to strike, pound, or beat

beatitude   **n.** supreme blessedness or happiness; Jesus' proclamations of blessedness in the "Sermon on the Mount"
"One of the Beatitudes from the Gospel of Matthew is 'Blessed are the peacemakers, for they shall be called children of God.'"
beatitudo blessedness < *beatus* blessed

rebellious   **adj.** showing a desire to rebel; resisting control, unruly
"A mutiny is a rebellious uprising to wrest command from a ship's captain."
re- back, again (expressing repetition) + *bellum* war

imbibe   **v.** to drink (usually alcohol); to absorb (knowledge, ideas, etc.)
"Seventh Day Adventists do not imbibe alcoholic drinks of any kind."
imbibere drink in, absorb: *im-* in + *bibere* to drink

abbreviation   **n.** the act or product of shortening; a shortened form of a word
"Etc. is an abbreviation for the Latin words 'et cetera,' meaning 'and so on.'"
abbreviare: to shorten, cut off < *brevis, breve* brief, short

brevity   **n.** concise and exact use of words; the quality of being brief
"The Gettysburg Address, which lasted only a few minutes, was a marvel of brevity."
brevis, breve brief, short

casualty   **n.** a person killed or injured in a war or accident
"It is said that in war the first casualty is the truth."
casus fall, accident, emergency

recalcitrant   **adj.** obstinately uncooperative
"The recalcitrant child stubbornly refused to obey the rules."
recalcitrance (n.)
recalcitrare to be disobedient, kick out with the heels < *calx, calcis* heel

candid   **adj.** truthful and straightforward; frank
"Let's be candid, instead of beating around the bush."
candidus transparent, white

candidate   n. a person who applies for a job or is nominated for election; a person or thing suitable for or likely to receive a particular fate, treatment, or position
"A scholar with strong social and leadership skills, he was a perfect candidate for university president."
candidatus white-robed < *candidus* white, transparent

incantation   n. a series of words said as a magic spell or in a ritual
"'Abracadabra' is the stage magician's standard incantation."
incantatory (adj.)
incantare to chant, to bewitch < *cantare* to sing

capture   v. to take possession of or to control; to seize by force; to arrest
"The blurry photograph failed to capture her true beauty."
capere to seize, to take

participate   v. to share; to take part in
"Patriots dressed as Indians participated in the Boston Tea Party."
participatory (adj.)
participare to take part in: *pars, part-* part + *capere* to take

Exercise A

Use the word box at the beginning of the lesson to fill in the blanks below:

1. The Buddhist monk radiated the _____ of one who has attained liberation from desire, pain and suffering.

2. The radio requires either a _____ or an AC adapter for power.

3. The substitute teacher's pleas for order were barely _____ over the students' chatter.

4. The American _____ uses a combination of infantry, armored vehicles, and tactical weapons during combat.

5. The Dave Matthews Band performed before an enthusiastic _____ on Saturday.

6. Pottery and arrowheads were some of the most valuable _____ found at the prehistoric village.

7. The silk flowers in the arrangement, although _____, are still attractive.

8. Joan's uncle Herb, her guardian since her father had died, met with Joan before her wedding to dispense a bit of _____ advice.

9. The school raised enough money to build a new _____ for plays and concerts.

10. Although a soldier may not be a _____ of war in the traditional sense, the psychological damage he suffers may cause life-long hardship.

11. The _____ for the United States of America is simply U.S.A.

12. A _____ photo is one that is natural, not posed.

13. Helen Keller was extremely _____ as a young child; it took the genius of Annie Sullivan to understand that Helen was protesting her inability to comprehend the world around her and communicate with others.

14. Jessica surprised the audience with the _____ of her song, which lasted only thirty seconds.

15. Choosing a _____ for each party is the purpose of the primary elections.

16. As Gandalf spoke the _____, the wind swirled and the earth shook menacingly.

17. It is illegal for people under 21 to _____ alcoholic beverages in most states.

18. In *The Catcher in the Rye*, Holden Caulfield is portrayed as a depressed and _____ teenager.

19. The Greeks were able to _____Troy by withdrawing most of their forces, but leaving an apparent gift outside the city gates: a huge wooden horse containing soldiers, who opened the city gates after the Trojans dragged the horse inside.

20. In high school, Britney Spears _____ in varsity basketball and other sports.

Exercise B

Match the word with the letter of its definition:

1. ____ abbreviation
2. ____ army
3. ____ artifact
4. ____ artificial
5. ____ audible
6. ____ audience
7. ____ auditorium
8. ____ avuncular
9. ____ battery
10. ____ beatitude
11. ____ brevity
12. ____ casualty
13. ____ candid
14. ____ candidate
15. ____ capture
16. ____ imbibe
17. ____ incantation
18. ____ participate
19. ____ rebellious
20. ____ recalcitrant

a) a man-made object
b) honest and frank
c) a theater or hall
d) the quality of being concise
e) injury purposefully inflicted on someone else
f) to approach or enter
g) a shortened form of a word
h) to take part in
i) able to be heard
j) a magic spell
k) supreme blessedness or happiness
l) to drink
m) an organized military force
n) a person or thing killed or injured, usually in war
o) spectators
p) unruly
q) kindly, like an uncle
r) obstinate
s) a job applicant or nominated official
t) unnatural

Exercise C

ACROSS
4 Supreme blessedness or happiness
6 Obstinately uncooperative
8 Man-made or unnatural
10 A container consisting of one or more cells that produce electricity power
12 Truthful and straightforward; frank
14 A series of words said as a magic spell or in a ritual
18 To drink; to absorb
19 An object made by a human being

DOWN
1 Showing a desire to go against authority
2 The act or product of shortening
3 Being kind and friendly towards a younger person
4 Concise and exact use of words
5 To take part in
7 A person who applies for a job or is nominated for election
9 The assembled spectators at an event
11 The part of a theater or hall in which an audience sits
13 Able to be heard
15 A person killed or injured in a war or accident
16 To take possession of or to control; to seize by force
17 An organized military force

Lesson VIII

CAPUT, CARN-, CASTIG-, CEREBRUM, CERN-, CED-,
CELER, CENS-, CENT-, CID-, CIT-, CIVIS

CAPUT head	CARN- flesh; meat	CASTIG- to punish	CEREBRUM brain	CERN- to separate	CED- to yield, go
CELER fast	CENS- to assess	CENT- one hundred	CID-, CIS- to cut, kill	CIT, CITAL to start, call	CIVIS citizen

> *decapitate, carnivorous, castigate, cerebral, discern,*
> *access, accessory, accelerate, decelerate, censor, census,*
> *centennial, century, concise, incision, excite, incite, civil,*
> *civilian, civilization*

Word Definitions

decapitate
v. to cut off the head
"The guillotine decapitated scores of aristocrats – as well as its inventor."
decapitation (n.)
decapitare to decapitate: *de-* away + *caput, capitis* head

carnivorous
adj. of an animal feeding on meat or other animal life
"Unlike the brachiosaurus, whose diet consisted entirely of plants, the tyrannosaurus rex was carnivorous."
carnivorus eating flesh: *caro, carnis* flesh + *vorare* to devour

castigate
v. to reprimand or punish severely
"Horrible machines of torture castigated medieval prisoners."
castigation (n.)
castigare to punish, to correct < *castus* pure, chaste

cerebral
adj. of the brain; intellectual rather than physical or emotional
"A scholar's work is cerebral rather than physical."
cerebrum brain

discernment
n. the ability to see something that tends to blend into its surroundings; the ability to understand despite obfuscation or confusion
discern (v.)
"Thanks to his powers of discernment, he is able to diagnose psychiatric patients quickly, even when they are uncooperative or difficult."
discernere to discern or distinguish: *dis-* apart + *cernere* to separate

access   **n.** the means or opportunity to approach or enter a place
"Only men and male animals get access to Mt. Athos monastery."
v. to approach or enter (a place); to retrieve information stored in a computer
"Joe was able to access the stairway because the door was not locked."
accedere to approach, add to: *ad-* toward + *cedere* to give way, yield

accessory   **n.** A supplement or object which can be added to something else, making it more useful, versatile, or attractive; a person who helps a criminal
"Chris thought the dress very plain, but the sales clerk showed her how a couple of accessories, such as a jazzy handbag and belt, could dress it up."
adj. subsidiary or supplementary
"That application is accessory to the payroll software, but you don't need it."
accedere to approach, add to: *ad-* toward + *cedere* to give way, yield

accelerate   **v.** to speed up
"The spread of a fire can be accelerated with gasoline."
acceleration (n.)
accelerare to hasten: *ad-* toward + *celerare* to move quickly < *celer* swift, quick

decelerate   **v.** to slow down
"Brakes decelerate a moving vehicle and bring it to a stop."
deceleration (n.)
de- away + *celerare* to move quickly < *celer* swift, quick

censor   **n.** an official who examines material before publication in order to suppress parts deemed offensive or a threat to security
"The censor must do his job right in order to protect the public from vulgar language."
v. to examine (a book, film, etc.) and suppress portions of it
"In the United States, the government may not censor news stories before publication unless it can persuade a judge that a story poses an extreme and immediate threat to life."
censere to assess or judge

census   **n.** an official count or survey of a population
"The U.S. Constitution mandates a census every decade to ensure that each congressional district represents about the same number of people."
censere to assess or judge

centennial   **n.** a century; the completion or celebration of a 100-year period
"The Centennial International Exhibition, the first official world's fair, was held in Philadelphia in 1876 to mark the hundredth anniversary of the signing of the Declaration of Independence."
adj. marking the completion of 100 years
"The centennial celebration of Custer's last stand occurred in 1976, when the United States was celebrating its bicentennial as a nation."
centum one hundred

century **n.** a period of one hundred years
"The century plant blooms roughly every hundred years."
centum one hundred

concise **adj.** giving information clearly and in a few words
"A concise history of the flea: 'Adam had 'em.'"
concision (n.)
concidere to cut down; to collapse: *con-* against + *caedere* to cut, to kill

incision **n.** a surgical cut
"The surgeon was nervous about making the incision, for she knew if her cut was even a centimeter off, she risked the patient's life."
incidere to cut into: *in-* in + *caedere* to cut

excite **v.** to cause to feel enthusiastic and eager; to awaken or arouse
"She tried to excite his interest, but he was so tired he couldn't focus on what she was saying."
excitare to excite: *ex-* out + *citare* to rouse, to call

incite **v.** to encourage or stir up
"Revere, Prescott, and Dawes incited the colonists to take up arms."
incitation (n.)
incitare: in- toward + *citare* to rouse, to call

civil **adj.** relating to ordinary citizens, as distinct from military, religious, or criminal matters; courteous and polite
"Civil courts decide lawsuits between businesses or individuals; criminal courts hear cases involving crimes."
civis citizen

civilian **n.** a person not in the armed services or the police force
"The army general was happy to retire and live as a civilian again."
adj. relating to citizens
"When on leave at home, soldiers are required to wear civilian clothes, or 'civvies,' instead of their uniforms."
civis citizen

civilization **n.** an advanced stage or system of human social development; a particular culture or society
"Ancient Greek civilization is credited with advancing the arts, sciences, philosophy, and mathematics."
civis citizen

Exercise A

Use the word box at the beginning of the lesson to fill in the blanks below:

1. Although all dogs are _____ by nature, real meat is still a treat for most pets.

2. The detective's _____ helped him sort out the important clues from the mass of witness statements, forensic evidence, and crime scene photographs.

3. Islamic extremists have been known to _____ their hostages.

4. Her father _____ Susan for going to the movies the night before her math test, instead of studying.

5. The world's tallest man grew to a height of 8'4" because of slight _____ damage he suffered during brain surgery.

6. Only highly trusted employees have _____ to casino vaults.

7. The town conducted an annual _____ using property and tax records to determine whether its population was growing or shrinking.

8. Although computers have become less expensive, the prices of optional _____ have remained the same or gone up.

9. A fully loaded tractor-trailer can maintain its speed on a slight incline, but _____ when climbing steeper hills.

10. In China, the government tries to _____ any discussion of opposing political views, but cell phones and the internet have made it difficult to stifle all dissent.

11. To get through the intersection before the light turned red, the sports car had to _____.

12. The doctors made a small _____ in Daniel's abdomen to extract the bullet from his spleen.

13. The fifth _____ A.D. saw the fall of the Roman Empire, one of the greatest civilizations on Earth.

14. The Yankee fan's verbal abuse of the Red Sox player _____ a riot in the bleachers.

15. The attacks of Sept. 11, 2001, caused more _____ casualties than any previous terrorist attack against the United States.

16. Her brief, _____ speech was well received by the audience, which was weary of long-winded politicians.

17. A 1997 book celebrates the _____ of Queen Victoria's Silver Jubilee in 1897, which included ceremonies intended to demonstrate the British Empire's power.

18. Chinese _____ was flourishing when Europe, ravaged by the bubonic plague, entered the Dark Ages.

19. Merely the thought of the upcoming basketball season was enough to _____ Tom Nicholson, a die-hard Lakers fan.

20. The U.S. Supreme Court has the responsibility of protecting the _____ rights of all citizens, including criminals.

Exercise B

Match the word with the letter of its definition:

1. ____ access
2. ____ accessory
3. ____ accelerate
4. ____ carnivorous
5. ____ castigate
6. ____ censor
7. ____ census
8. ____ cerebral
9. ____ centennial
10. ____ century
11. ____ civil
12. ____ civilian
13. ____ civilization
14. ____ concise
15. ____ decapitate
16. ____ decelerate
17. ____ discernment
18. ____ excite
19. ____ incision
20. ____ incite

a) eating only meat
b) someone who monitors and suppresses unacceptable speech
c) one-hundredth anniversary
d) relating to ordinary citizens
e) an advanced system of human development
f) to approach or enter
g) the ability to make fine distinctions
h) a surgical cut
i) to reprimand severely
j) a supplementary item
k) to stir up or cause to act
l) of the brain; intellectual
m) a period of one hundred years
n) to cut off the head
o) someone not in the military
p) to speed up
q) an official count of population
r) to slow down
s) expressed clearly and in a few words
t) to arouse; to awaken

Exercise C

ACROSS
2. a period of one hundred years
3. an official count or survey of a population
5. examine (a book, film, etc.) and suppress portions of it
6. to cause to feel enthusiastic and eager
7. a person not in the armed services or the police force
9. to encourage or stir up
12. to cut off the head
15. of the brain
16. a surgical cut
17. to reprimand or punish severely
18. the ability to see something that tends to blend into its surroundings

DOWN
1. to slow down
4. giving information clearly and in a few words
5. an advanced stage or system of human social development
7. of an animal feeding on meat or other animal life
8. subsidiary or supplementary
10. marking the completion of 100 years
11. courteous and polite
13. to speed up
14. the means or opportunity to approach or enter a place

Lesson IX

CLAM-, CLAR-, CLAUD-, CLIN-, COGNIT-, COLLUM,
COMPL-, COPIA, COR, CORPUS, CRED-

CLAM- to cry out	*CLAR-* clear	*CLAUD-* to close, shut	*CLIN-* to slope, bend
COGNIT- to learn	*COLLUM* neck	*COMPL-* to fill	*COPIA* plenty
COR heart	*CORPUS, CORPOR-* body	*CRED-* believe	

acclaim, clarity, clarify, cloister, closure, enclosure, recluse, decline, inclined, cognition, incognito, accolade, complement, comply, copious, cordial, corpse, incorporate, creditable, creed

Word Definitions

acclaim
v. to praise enthusiastically and publicly
"Lindberg was acclaimed for his solo Atlantic flight."
n. widespread public praise
"Steven Spielberg's films have garnered critical and popular acclaim."
acclamare to shout approval: *ad-* to + *clamare* to shout out or proclaim

clarity
n. the state or quality of being clear, distinct, and easily perceived or understood; transparency
"Even at age 90, the scholar showed great clarity of mind."
clarus clear

clarify
v. to make more comprehensible; to separate out impurities
clarification (n.)
"Butter is clarified by heating it and skimming off the milk solids."
clarus clear

cloister
n. a covered, and typically colonnaded, passage round an open court in a convent, monastery, college, or cathedral
"A medieval woman's choice was marriage or the cloister."
v. to seclude or shut up in a convent, monastery or other secluded place
"He cloistered himself in a solitary cabin while he completed his novel."
claustrum or *claustri* cloister < *claudere* or *cludere* to shut or close

closure   **n.** the act or process of closing; a feeling that turmoil from a troubling experience has been resolved
"The divorce decree signaled closure for their marriage, but not their relationship as parents."
claudere or *cludere* to shut or close

enclosure   **n.** an area that is sealed off by a barrier; a document or object placed in an envelope together with a letter
"Although they were refugees, the government held them in a barbed wire enclosure so they would not mix with the local population and settle there."
includere or *inclaudere* to shut in: *in-* in + *claudere* to shut or close

recluse   **n.** a person who avoids others and lives a solitary life; a hermit
reclusive (adj.)
"A hermit disdains company and lives as a recluse."
recludere to enclose: *re-* again + *cludere* to shut or close

decline   **v.** to become smaller, fewer, or less; to decrease; to say no to
"They declined the invitation because they were ill."
n. a continuous loss of strength, numbers, or value; a downward slope
"After a steady decline in sales, the store had to lay off some employees."
declinare to bend down, turn aside: *de-* down + *clinare* to bend or slope

inclined   **v.** to be favorably disposed toward or willing to do; sloping or leaning
"I was not inclined to agree with his radical viewpoint."
inclinare to bend or lower: *in-* toward + *clinare* to bend or slope

cognition   **n.** the mental action or process of acquiring knowledge through thought, experience, and the senses
cognitive (adj.)
"His cognition was impaired after he suffered a concussion."
cognoscere to learn or recognize

incognito   **adj. & adv.** with one's true identity concealed
"To escape their fans, Hollywood stars often travel incognito."
n. an assumed or false identity
"Once the secret agent's incognito was uncovered, he had to change his appearance and alias."
in- not, against + *cognoscere* to learn or recognize

accolade   **n.** something granted as a special honor or in recognition of merit; applause; a touch on the shoulder with a sword that is part of the knighthood ceremony
"The Nobel Prize for Literature is the highest literary accolade."
ad- to, toward + *collum* neck

complement   **v.** to add something that enhances or improves (something else)
"Her vision and his business ability complemented each other nicely."
n. a thing that adds to and completes something else; the opposite of something else (in a positive sense)
"In Chinese philosophy, Yin is the complement to Yang."

comply	*complere* to fill up, finish, fulfill: *com-* together + *plere* to fill **v.** to act in accordance with a wish or command; to meet specified standards "Even the president must comply with the law." *complere* to fill up, finish, fulfill: *com-* together + *plere* to fill
copious	**adj.** abundant in quantity or supply "He is a diligent student who he takes copious notes in class." *copia* plenty
cordial	**adj.** warm and friendly; strongly felt "The diplomat extended a cordial welcome to her guests." **n.** a post-dinner liqueur "Many Italian restaurants serve cordials after dinner." *cor-, cordis* heart, mind, or spirit
corpse	**n.** a dead body, especially human "While hiking in the backcountry, he stumbled across a decaying corpse." *corpus* body
incorporate	**v.** to take in or include as part of a whole; to constitute as a legal corporation "The two Andovers decided to incorporate as a single town." *in-* into + *corporare* to make or form into a body < *corpus* body
creditable	**adj.** competent, but not necessarily outstanding "The applicant had a creditable but undistinguished work history." *credere* to believe, to trust
creed	**n.** a system of belief; a religious doctrine "The creed of the jungle is kill or be killed." *credere* to believe, to trust

Exercise A

Use the word box at the beginning of the lesson to fill in the blanks below:

1. The _____ protected the monks from rain and snow as they walked between the chapel and the dining hall, offices, and cells.

2. He asked his teacher to _____ several points so he could understand the theory.

3. After adjusting the microscope carefully, Peter could see the parasite with great _____.

4. Her Carnegie Hall premiere was greeted with critical _____.

5. Years after her son's sudden death, she dedicated a playground in his memory, which helped her achieve a sense of _____.

6. During the winter, the sheep exercised in an _____ near the barn.

7. She was initially _____ to vote for Hillary Clinton in the Democratic primary, but changed her mind at the last minute and cast her ballot for Barack Obama.

8. Lindsay wished she could _____ the invitation, but her publicist said she could start rehabilitating her image by going to the party and staying sober.

9. The United States was asked to _____ with the Geneva Conventions on human rights during the invasion and occupation of Iraq.

10. He drank _____ amounts of water, but it did nothing to abate his hunger.

11. After a sterling performance, Jerome received the highest _____: first prize and the opportunity to perform his concerto with the Boston Symphony Orchestra.

12. Illustrations should _____ the author's text.

13. Research on _____ has helped psychologists devise more effective strategies for helping patients with phobias, obsessive thinking, and depression.

14. James Bond, even though he is a spy, operates openly and rarely goes _____.

15. Although he is publicly _____ to the former Green Party presidential candidate, privately Al Gore feels nothing but bitterness toward Ralph Nader.

16. To capture the attention of the class, the math teacher sought to _____ rap music into his multimedia presentation of integrals.

17. "Practice makes perfect" is the personal _____ of Jerry Rice, perhaps the greatest football player ever to grace the gridiron.

18. The Egyptians were able to preserve the _____ of their pharaohs by mummifying their remains.

19. Her proposal was thorough and _____, but not particularly original or inspired.

20. After his wife's death, he declined all invitations to golf or dinner, had his groceries delivered, stopped answering his phone, and became a _____.

Exercise B

Match the word with the letter of its definition:

1. ____ acclaim
2. ____ accolade
3. ____ clarify
4. ____ clarity
5. ____ cloister
6. ____ closure
7. ____ cognition
8. ____ complement
9. ____ comply
10. ____ copious
11. ____ cordial
12. ____ corpse
13. ____ creditable
14. ____ creed
15. ____ decline
16. ____ enclosure
17. ____ inclined
18. ____ incognito
19. ____ incorporate
20. ____ recluse

a) to decrease; to refuse
b) articles of faith
c) warm and friendly
d) to meet specified standards
e) a covered walkway; to seclude in an abbey or monastery
f) anonymously
g) to separate out the impurities; to clear up
h) the process of thinking
i) a dead body
j) praise
k) transparency
l) to fit well with something else
m) competent, but not outstanding
n) a high honor
o) to take in; to include
p) a feeling of resolution
q) a hermit
r) abundant
s) leaning toward (something)
t) something placed in an envelope with a letter

Exercise C

ACROSS
3 To be favorably disposed toward or willing to do
7 An assumed or false identity
8 The act or process of closing
9 Warm and friendly; an after-dinner liqueur
11 A thing that enhances and completes something else
12 A dead body, especially human
15 Something granted as a special honor or in recognition of merit
16 A covered, and typically colonnaded, passage round an open court
17 To act in accordance with a wish or command

DOWN
1 To praise enthusiastically and publicly
2 To set up as a corporation
4 An area that is surrounded by a barrier

5   Abundant; plentiful
6   A person who avoids other and lives a solitary life; a hermit
9   Deserving public acknowledgement
10 A system of belief; a religious doctrine
11 The mental action or process of acquiring knowledge
12 The quality of being clear
13 To become smaller, fewer, or less; to decrease
14 To make clear or distinct

Lesson X

CRESC-, CRUCIS, CUMB-, CULPA, CUPI-, CURR-, DA-,
DENS, DICT-, DOC-, DOMIN-

CRESC-	CRUCIS	CUMB-	CULPA	CUPI-	CURR-
to grow	cross	to lie down	fault, guilt	to desire	to run

DA-	DENS, DENTIS	DICT-	DOC-	DOMIN-
to give	tooth	to say	to teach	to rule

> *crescendo, accrue, cruciform, incumbent, succumb, culpable, cupidity concur, curriculum, data, mandate, indentation, trident, dictator, diction, verdict, docile, domestic, dominant, domain*

Word Definitions

crescendo **n.** a gradual increase in volume in a piece of music; the peak of such loudness
"*The 1812 Overture* ends with a crescendo of cannons and bells."
crescere to grow, to increase

accrue **v.** (of a benefit or sum of money) to grow through regular increases or additions
"Over the years, a savings bond accrues annual interest."
accrual (n.)
accrescere to grow: *ad-* to + *crescere* to grow

cruciform **adj.** having the shape of a cross
"The ankh is a looped, cruciform symbol of life dating from ancient Egypt."
crux, cruc- cross + *forma* shape

incumbent **adj.** required of (someone) as a duty or responsibility
"It is incumbent upon a soldier to obey the orders of his superior."
n. the current holder of a post or elective office

61

"Barack Obama is the incumbent president."
incumbere to lean forward; to press on < *cubare* to lie on

succumb **v.** to fail to resist (pleasure, temptation, etc.); to die from the effect of a disease or injury; to yield or to give in
"Eve succumbed to the serpent's suggestion that she eat the forbidden fruit."
succumbere to collapse or surrender: *sub-* under + *cubare* to lie

culpable **adj.** deserving blame; guilty
"Pamela Smart was culpable in her husband's murder, even though she wasn't present when her teenage lover shot him."
culpability (n.)
culpare to blame

cupidity **n.** greed for money or possessions
"King Midas's name is synonymous with cupidity."
cupere to desire

concur **v.** to agree; to happen at the same time
"We can't begin until all parties concur on the plan."
concurrence (n.)
concurrere to run together or agree: *con-* together + *currere* to run

curriculum **n.** the subjects comprising a course of study in a school or college
"The pre-med curriculum is very challenging."
curricular (adj.)
curriculum race course or racing chariot; course of action < *currere* to run

data **n.** facts, statistics, and other items of information
"His experiment did not yield enough data to draw meaningful conclusions."
datum something given < *dare* to give

mandate **v.** to require (something) or give (someone) authority to do something
"Hospital policy mandates that instruments be sterilized."
n. an official order or commission to do something; (in politics) strong approval for a course of action, presumed from wide margin of victory in an election
"The Democratic sweep of the presidency and both houses of Congress gave them a mandate to push through health care reform."
mandare to commission or command: *manus* hand + *dare* to give

indentation **n.** the action of indenting or the state of being indented; setting inward from the margin
"A small indentation marked where a shotgun pellet had struck the car."
indentare to cut into teeth: *en-, in-* into + *dens, dentis* tooth

trident **n.** a three-pronged spear
"Some gladiators used the trident and net as weapons."

tri- three + *dens, dentis* tooth

dictator n. a ruler with total power over a country or institution
"Hitler became a dictator after suspending most democratic rights."
dictare to say repeatedly; to prescribe or order

diction n. the choice and use of words in speech or writing; enunciation
"When writing a formal essay, it is important not to use colloquial diction."
dicere to say

verdict n. a final decision on the facts in a civil or criminal case, or at an inquest
"A jury is charged with rendering a verdict of guilt or innocence."
verus true + *dictum* saying

docile adj. easily taught or managed; of an easy, compliant temperament
"The tutor was happy to teach the eager, docile pupils."
docere to teach

domestic adj. relating to the home, family, or other matters near one's home; (in government) pertaining to national affairs (as opposed to international issues)
"The president hired new advisors to counsel him on domestic problems."
n. a household servant
"The Industrial Revolution offered employment and independence to many workers who, in earlier times, would have sought work as domestics."
domus house

dominant adj. ruling or governing; occupying a commanding position or influence; major
"The New York Yankees are generally the dominant team in the American League East, although the Boston Red Sox have sometimes bested them."
dominare to be master of, to rule over < *domus* house

domain n. (1) a territory where someone or something has influence or control
"No one can leave the king's domain."
n. (2) a sphere of activity, concern, or focus
"The tenured professor's domain was ancient Chinese history."
dominare to be master of, to rule over < *domus* house

Exercise A

Use the word box at the beginning of the lesson to fill in the blanks below:

1. Ravel's stirring orchestral piece, *Bolero,* is one long, gradual _____.

2. No man could resist _____ to the sirens' call, despite its portent of doom.

3. The boy's parents weren't found guilty of the crimes he had committed, but many people considered them equally _____ because they had abused and neglected him.

4. Most Christian churches are built in a _____ shape.

5. The _____ mayor had two years remaining in his term.

6. The stockbroker's _____ eventually led him to steal from his clients.

7. Until he discovered an old IBM stock certificate in his attic, Enrique did not fully appreciate how an investment could _____ value over time.

8. It's a dire mistake to confuse a feral wolf with a _____ husky.

9. Coach Bill Parcells used fines to enforce his _____ that his players treat him and the staff with respect at all times.

10. MCAS tests, required for high school graduation, are part an attempt to standardize the _____ of Massachusetts public schools.

11. Sadly, many people confuse the splendor of Poseidon's _____ with the wickedness of the devil's pitchfork.

12. Although Stephen Hawking was fascinated by Homer Simpson's idea of a doughnut-shaped universe, Simpson had no _____ to support his theory.

13. It is rare for everyone to _____ with the president's policies, but most members of his party go along, in exchange for his support of their pet projects.

14. An _____ signifying a new paragraph should be used in written dialogue each time the speaker changes.

15. Even though she did well in school and her parents wanted her to go to college, she secretly dreamed of getting married, having children, and settling into a quiet, _____ life.

16. While the legal powers of the royal family have been supplanted by a parliamentary government, the British Isles are still considered the queen's _____.

17. His right hand is his _____ hand, but occasionally he bats lefty just to rattle the opposing pitcher.

18. Young writing students sometimes over-use imagery and metaphor while ignoring _____, the most powerful tool a writer has in setting a tone.

19. Kobe Bryant's reputation will be forever tainted by the sex scandal in Colorado, regardless of the _____ reached by the jury in his trial.

20. Fidel Castro, the former _____ of Cuba, openly aided the Soviet Union and its satellites during the cold war.

Exercise B
Match the word with the letter of its definition:

1. ____ accrue
2. ____ concur
3. ____ crescendo
4. ____ cruciform
5. ____ culpable
6. ____ cupidity
7. ____ curriculum
8. ____ data
9. ____ dictator
10. ____ diction
11. ____ docile
12. ____ domain
13. ____ domestic
14. ____ dominant
15. ____ incumbent
16. ____ indentation
17. ____ mandate
18. ____ succumb
19. ____ trident
20. ____ verdict

a) controlling; most powerful
b) manner or clarity of speech
c) an area under control
d) a three-pronged weapon
e) to increase or add to over time
f) shaped like a cross
g) a household servant
h) the space set in from the margin of a document
i) a course of study
j) to agree
k) information for analysis
l) to demand action
m) a steady increase in volume
n) the current holder of a public office or post
o) submissive
p) extreme desire for riches
q) an absolute ruler
r) to yield; to give in to
s) deserving blame
t) a jury's decision

Exercise C

ACROSS
2. Greed for money or possessions
5. A gradual increase in volume in a piece of music
6. To fail to resist pleasure, temptation, etc.
7. Required as a duty or responsibility
8. Deserving blame; guilty
11. The subjects comprising a course of study in a school
12. Most important, powerful, or influential
14. To agree; to happen at the same time
15. A three-pronged spear
16. An area owned or controlled by a ruler or government
17. An official order or commission to do something

5 Having the shape of a cross
9 Relating to the home or family affairs
10 A final decision on the facts in a civil or criminal case
12 The choice and use of words in speech or writing
13 Willing to be taught or guided
18 Facts, statistics and other items of information

DOWN
1 To grow through regular increases or additions
3 The action of indenting or the state of being indented; a pockmark
4 A ruler with total power over a country or institution

Quiz 2

agility, civilization, alienated, amateur, verdict, corpse, incumbent, recluse, carnivorous, annuity, aptitude, amiable, acrid, artifacts, incorporate, agitate, inept, copious, crescendo, civilian, acute

1. In the Vietnam War, bombing tactics were inefficient and thus many _____ were killed.

2. The _____ in the infamous Casey Anthony trial was "not guilty."

3. Here in the tutoring office, we have a _____ supply of legal pads to write on.

4. When Howard Carter discovered the remains of King Tut in 1922, the world was amazed by the splendor of all the Ancient Egyptian _____.

5. The boy genius was _____ from the other college students by his age, but his professors considered him an _____ kid.

6. Because of a police dog's _____ sense of smell, it can detect human _____ even when their scent is obscured by _____ chemical fumes.

7. The _____ lived alone for many years, but then he befriended the priest in the nearby town, who encouraged him to _____ himself into the community.

8. The earliest signs of _____ can be found in Mesopotamia, the land between the Tigris and Euphrates Rivers.

9. Although the gymnast was an _____, she performed better than most professionals, amazing the crowd with her _____.

10. The power of financial compounding can be seen in an _____.

11. From an early age, the writer showed an _____ for creative expression.

12. Swimmers in Australian waters must take caution not to _____ predatory, _____ animals like great white sharks.

13. "*The din became a _____, like the roar of an oncoming train.*" - *The Red Badge of Courage*

14. The _____ faces a tough reelection battle next November.

15. Despite standing 7 feet tall, the European basketball player proved _____ as the team's starting center because he wasn't fast enough to keep up with the smaller players.

Lesson XI

DORMI-, DORSUM, EGO, EQU-, ERR-, FAC-, FACIES,
FALL-, FER-, FERV-, FIDES, FINIS, FING-

DORMI- to sleep	*DORSUM* back	*EGO* I	*EQU-* equal	*ERR-* to wander	*FAC-* to make, do
FACIES face	*FALL-* to deceive	*FER-* to bring, bear	*FERV-* to boil	*FIDES* belief, faith	*FINIS* end

FING-
to shape

---

dormant, endorse, egocentric, equal, erratic, erroneous, facsimile, fiction, deface, façade, falsify, infallible, confer, fertile, fervor, fidelity, affinity, finite, configuration, figurative

---

Word Definitions

dormant **adj.** in or seeming to be in a deep sleep; inactive
"A long dormant affection for the girl next door finally awakened when he reached adulthood."
dormire to sleep

endorse **v.** to declare one's public approval of (someone or something); to sign a check on the back
"Sports stars are paid millions to endorse and promote athletic products."
endorsement (n.)
in- on, upon + *dorsum* back

egocentric	**adj.** self-centered "He who acts as if the world revolves around himself is egocentric." *egocentricity (n.)* *ego* I + *kentron* (Greek for center)
equal	**adj.** being the same in quantity, size, degree, value, or status "One hundred pennies is equal in value to a dollar bill." **n.** a person or thing that is equal to another "As a piano virtuoso, Mozart had no equal." *equality (n.)* *aequus* even, level, equal
erratic	**adj.** uneven or irregular in pattern or movement "A performance that is not consistent and predictable is erratic." *errare* to wander; to err
erroneous	**adj.** wrong; incorrect "His logic was faulty, so his conclusions were erroneous." *errare* to wander; to err
facsimile	**n.** an exact copy of written or printed matter "A fax machine scans documents and transmits their facsimiles to a distant machine." *facere* to do, to make + *similis* like
fiction	**n.** prose literature, especially novels; a thing that is invented, untrue "Investigation proved the senator's claim of military service to be a fiction." *fictitious (adj.)* *fictus* formed; created; invented < *fingere* to shape; to contrive
deface	**v.** to spoil the surface or appearance of; to mar or disfigure "The vandals defaced the gravestones with red spray paint." *de-* (expressing reversal) + *facies* face
façade	**n.** the decorative front of a building, facing the street; a deceptive appearance "The smile was a façade that masked his deep sorrow." *facies* face
falsify	**v.** to alter so as to mislead; to make false "A falsified signature on a tax form is grounds for imprisonment." *falsification (n.)* *falsificare* falsify: *falsus* false + *ficare* to make (variant of *facere*)
infallible	**adj.** incapable of making mistakes or being wrong; unfailing "Catholics believe the Pope is infallible because his pronouncements are inspired by God." *infallibility (n.)* *in-* not + *fallere* to deceive; to fail

confer
v. to grant a title, degree, benefit, or right
"Only the king or queen may confer knighthood on a deserving subject."
conferre to bring together, to gather: *con-* together + *ferre* to bring, to carry

fertile
adj. producing or capable of producing abundant growth (vegetation)
"The housing projects proved to be fertile ground for gangs."
fertility (n.)
ferre to bring, to carry

fervor
n. an intense and passionate feeling
"Jonathan Edwards' fervor erupted in hell-fire sermons."
fervere to boil; to be hot

fidelity
n. loyalty to a person, cause, or belief; resemblance to reality
"Early stereo record players were known as 'hi-fis' for their high degree of fidelity in reproducing the original musical performance."
fides faith

affinity
n. a spontaneous or natural liking or sympathy; a talent or leaning
"His affinity for animals made him an excellent veterinary technician."
affinis neighboring; related (inside the family): *ad-* toward + *finis* limit, boundary, end

finite
adj. limited in size or extent
"Though it is boundless, the universe contains a finite amount of matter."
finire to limit; to finish

configuration
n. an arrangement of parts or elements in a particular form or figure
"A baseball infield has a diamond-shaped configuration."
configure (v.)
configurare to shape after a pattern: *con-* together + *figurare* to shape

figurative
adj. (1) representing symbolically or by a figure; resembling
"The figurative sculpture of a broken window represented World War I."
adj. (2) characterized by figures of speech, especially metaphors; not literal
"He gave a figurative description of what happened to the officers."
figurativus, symbolic

Exercise A

Use the word box at the beginning of the lesson to fill in the blanks below:

1. Celebrity athletes often let their status go to their heads, becoming hopelessly _____ and acting as if others exist only to flatter and serve them.

2. McDonald's and Burger King are an _____ distance from our home, but we usually go to the "Home of the Whopper" because there's less traffic that way.

3. The city of Pompeii was built at the base of Mount Vesuvius, a volcano that had been considered

_____, but suddenly erupted after decades of inactivity.

4. The _____ comings and goings of the Mitfords caused much speculative talk in the village, as none of them appeared to hold a steady job.

5. The *New York Post* published an _____ report that John Kerry had chosen Dick Gephardt as his vice-presidential running mate.

6. John Kerry _____ Barack Obama over Hillary Clinton in the Democratic presidential primary.

7. Although Robin Hood wore a disguise to the archery contest, his expert marksmanship allowed the sheriff to see through the _____.

8. After the homecoming game victory, the _____ of the fans spilled over into a celebration on the field and an impromptu parade around campus.

9. When she traveled across Europe, Judith kept a _____ of her passport tucked into a separate bag, in case she lost the original.

10. It is likely that a Sufi monk tried to _____ the magnificent sphinx around 1100 A.D., as an insult to the Egyptian people.

11. Although Bill Gates once boasted that Windows XP would be _____, it proved to have as many bugs as its predecessors.

12. *To Kill A Mockingbird* is considered one of the greatest pieces of American _____, in part because the characters and plot are so realistic.

13. The teenager tried to _____ his age by tampering with his driver's license, but the bouncer spotted the fakery.

14. Nancy Kerrigan, like many competitive figure skaters, displayed an _____ for the sport at a young age.

15. A successful marriage must have a strong foundation of good communication and mutual _____.

16. He _____ a great honor on her when he chose her as chief operating officer.

17. The number of human beings that the earth can support is _____, although scientists do not agree on an exact figure.

18. The _____ valley of the Nile produces bountiful harvests.

19. Daniel's biting wit and clever use of _____ language caught the attention of Mr. Meade, his ninth-grade English teacher.

20. Astrologers believe that the _____ of the planets at a person's birth determines his or her unique personality.

Exercise B

Match the word with the letter of its definition:

1. ___ affinity
2. ___ confer
3. ___ configuration
4. ___ deface
5. ___ dormant
6. ___ egocentric
7. ___ endorse
8. ___ equal
9. ___ erratic
10. ___ erroneous
11. ___ façade
12. ___ facsimile
13. ___ falsify
14. ___ fervor
15. ___ fertile
16. ___ fiction
17. ___ fidelity
18. ___ figurative
19. ___ finite
20. ___ infallible

a) heightened passion
b) incorrect
c) to alter so as to mislead or make false
d) self-centered
e) to disfigure
f) an arrangement or pattern
g) a duplicate
h) to publicly support
i) prose literature that is not factual
j) having a limit
k) natural preference
l) using figures of speech
m) irregular
n) to consult with
o) foolproof
p) having the same value
q) asleep or inactive
r) loyalty
s) an illusion
t) capable of supporting abundant life

Exercise C

ACROSS
1. An exact copy of written or printed matter
3. To spoil the surface or appearance of
6. Decorative front of a building
8. Limited in size or extent
9. Self-centered
10. To declare one's public approval
11. To grant a title, degree, benefit, or right
12. An intense and passionate feeling
13. Being the same in quality, size, degree, value or status

14 A spontaneous or natural liking or sympathy
15 To alter so as to mislead; to make untrue
16 In or seeming to be in a deep sleep; inactive

DOWN
1   Creative prose literature
2   Incapable of making mistakes or being wrong
4   Wrong, incorrect
5   Producing or capable of producing abundant growth
6   Loyalty to a person, cause, or belief
7   An arrangement in a particular form
10 Uneven or irregular in pattern or movement

Lesson XII

FIRMUS, FLECT-, FLORIS, FLU-, FORS, FORUM, FRANG-, FRATER, FRONS, FUG-, FUS-, GURG-, GEN-

FIRMUS	*FLECT-*	*FLORIS*	*FLU-*	*FORS, FORTIS*	*FORUM*	*FRANG-*
strong	to bend	flower	to flow	luck	place	to break

FRATER	*FRONS*	*FUG-*	*FUS-*	*GURG-*	*GEN-, GENRE*
brother	front	to flee	to pour	throat	class, kind

> *confirm, infirmary, deflect, inflection, floral, fluid, fortunate, forum, fragment, fragile, fraternal, confront, fugitive, diffuse, fusion, gorge, generate, generous, genuine, genre*

Word Definitions

confirm   **v.** to establish the truth or correctness of (something)
"The timely arrival of the comet confirmed Halley's prediction from years earlier."
confirmation (n.)
confirmare to strengthen; to secure: *con-* together + *firmare* to strengthen

infirmary   **n.** a place within a larger institution for the care of those who are ill or injured; a hospital
"The outbreak of mononucleosis filled the beds of the college infirmary."
infirmus weak, sick: *in-* not + *firmus* firm, strong

deflect   **v.** to deviate or cause to deviate from a straight course
"The bullet was deflected by the wall and hit a bystander."

deflection (n.)
deflectere to deflect: *de-* from + *flectere* to bend

inflection   n. a change in the form of a word to express a grammatical function or attribute; specific pronunciation of a word or syllable
"One can tell the regional origins of a speaker based on his inflection."
inflectere to bend, to change: *in-* into + *flectere* to bend

floral   adj. involving or relating to flowers
"The tables were decorated with colorful floral arrangements."
flos, floris flower

fluid   n. a substance with no fixed shape that yields easily to pressure; a liquid or gas
"The amber fluid spilled out of the bottle and onto the floor."
adj. able to flow easily; not settled or stable
"The game is still fluid; either side could win."
fluidity (n.)
fluere to flow

fortunate   adj. favored by or involving good luck
"Those still in perfect health in their 80s are fortunate indeed."
fortune (n.)
fors, fortis luck, chance

forum   n. a meeting place or medium for an exchange of views
"PTA meetings constitute a forum for parents to air grievances and work with teachers to improve the school's performance."
forum out of doors

fragment   n. a small part broken off or detached
"The explosion sent scores of glass fragments flying through the air."
frangere to break

fragile   adj. easily broken or damaged
"The starving refugees looked terribly fragile."
frangere to break

fraternal   adj. of or like a brother(s)
"A club that admits males only is a fraternal organization."
fraternity (n.)
frater brother

confront   v. to stand or meet face to face
"A psychiatrist may help you to confront long-repressed emotions."
confrontation (n.)
confrontare to confront: *con-* with, together + *frons, frontis* face

fugitive   n. a person who has escaped from captivity or is in hiding
"Many fugitives head north through New Hampshire, hoping to reach the Canadian border before they are apprehended."

	adj. quick to disappear; fleeting
	"Fugitive shadows passed rapidly across the darkening sky."
	fugere to flee

diffuse
v. to spread over a wide area; to dilute
"He diffused the tension in the room by telling a joke."
adj. spread out over a wide area; lacking clarity
"He's a charming speaker, but unfortunately his attention is diffuse and he meanders along various tangents."
diffusus spread out, scattered: *de-* down, from + *fusus* poured (past participle of the verb *fundere* to pour; to melt)

fusion
n. the process or result of joining together into a unit; a reaction in which light atomic nuclei meld to form a heavier nucleus
"The fusion of nickel and chromium makes Nichrome coils."
fusus poured < *fundere* to pour; to melt (metal)

gorge
n. a steep, narrow valley or ravine; a ravine created by the flow of a river
"While hiking in the Grand Canyon, he fell into a small gorge and was never seen again."
v. to eat a large amount greedily
"The ravenous lions gorged themselves on the dead zebra."
gurges whirlpool; abyss < *gurgulio* throat; gullet

generate
v. to cause; to produce
"The shouting match over the controversial bill generated more heat than light."
generation (n.)
generare to beget; to father

generous
adj. freely giving more of something than is necessary or expected
"The teacher was generous with praise and encouragement."
generosity (n.)
generosus noble; magnanimous

genuine
adj. truly what it is said to be; authentic; sincere and honest
"The derringer was the genuine article, not a copy."
genus birth; descent; type

genre
n. a style or category of art or literature
"Poetry, drama, and novels represent different literary genres."
genere to bring forth; to bear < *genus* birth; descent or origin; family; type

Exercise A

Use the word box at the beginning of the lesson to fill in the blanks below:

1. The dancer's movements were _____ and graceful, even when she was doing something as ordinary as grocery shopping.

2. The wedding planner designed an intricate _____ arrangement for the head table.

3. His speech _____ my belief in the power of love to work miracles.

4. The linebacker tried to _____ Tom Brady's pass, but Troy Brown shifted direction and caught the ball anyway.

5. The army _____ was equipped to treat wounded soldiers and injured Iraqi civilians alike.

6. When the wind blew through the open window, the _____ vase fell from the shelf and shattered.

7. The philosopher used his college classroom as a _____ to test many of his controversial ideas, before subjecting them to the harsher criticism of his peers.

8. Her comical _____ belied the sad facts of her story.

9. The _____ hid in a dumpster for three days, surviving on leftovers in the garbage, until a police dog discovered him.

10. We were all _____ to graduate before the school lowered its standards and a degree became meaningless.

11. The boys had a _____ connection; they regarded each other as members of an extended family.

12. Archaeologists spend much of their time trying to piece together _____ of pottery to try and determine a vessel's shape and use.

13. The drunken teenager _____ the police officer and ended up getting charged with resisting arrest.

14. One classic example of chaos theory is that a drop of blue dye put into a beaker of water will never _____ through the liquid in the same pattern twice.

15. The Iron Chef's _____ of French cooking techniques with Asian ingredients and presentation created exciting and delicious new dishes.

16. The huge _____ known as the Grand Canyon was created by a combination of seismic activity and erosion by the Colorado River.

17. The _____ of science fiction has often predicted developments in science and technology.

18. Her parents are always very _____ with gifts for the holidays.

19. Although John McCain has voiced his support for President Bush, many experts believe his endorsement is not _____.

20. Nuclear plants can _____ enough electricity to power a sizeable city.

Exercise B

Match the word with the letter of its definition:

1. _____ confirm
2. _____ confront
3. _____ diffuse
4. _____ deflect
5. _____ floral
6. _____ fluid
7. _____ fortunate
8. _____ forum
9. _____ fragment
10. _____ fragile
11. _____ fraternal
12. _____ fugitive
13. _____ fusion
14. _____ generate
15. _____ generous
16. _____ genre
17. _____ genuine
18. _____ gorge
19. _____ inflection
20. _____ infirmary

a) a piece of a whole
b) to face
c) a shapeless substance; a liquid or gas
d) a person who flees from the law
e) to cause to exist
f) a place for discussion
g) to spread over a wide area
h) favored by good luck
i) a steep valley; to eat greedily
j) freely giving
k) to acknowledge the truth of
l) to turn (something) aside
m) consisting of or relating to flowers
n) brotherly
o) easily breakable
p) the modulation of intonation in the voice
q) a hospital within a larger institution
r) authentic
s) a joining together
t) a category

Exercise C

ACROSS
3 To stand or meet face to face; to face down
6 Favored by or involving good luck
7 A substance that has no fixed shape; a liquid or gas
8 A person who has escaped from captivity or is in hiding
10 A place within a larger institution for the care of the ill or injured
13 To deviate or cause to deviate from a straight course
15 Freely giving more than is necessary or expected

17 Spread out over a wide area
18 A style or category of art or literature

19 A meeting place or medium for an exchange of views

DOWN
1 A change in the form of a word to express a grammatical function

2 Easily broken or damaged
4 The process or result of joining together into a unit
5 Of or like a brother(s)
6 A small part broken off or detached
9 To cause; to produce
11 Truly what it is said to be
12 Relating to or consisting of flowers
14 To establish the truth or correctness of
16 A steep, narrow valley or ravine

Lesson XIII

GRAD-, GRAT-, GREGIS, HER-, IMPEL-, INCEND-,
IRA, ITER-, JAC-, JOCUS, JUDIC-, JUNCT-

| *GRAD-, GRESS* | *GRAT-* | *GREGIS* | *HER-, HES-* |
| go; step; advance | please; favor | flock, herd | to stick |

| *IMPEL-* | *INCEND-* | *IRA* | *ITER-, ITINE-* |
| drive; persuade | to set on fire | anger | journey; road |

| *JAC-, JEC-* | *JOCUS* | *JUDIC-* | *JUNCT-, JUG-* |
| to throw | joke | to judge | to join |

gradual, graduate, ingredient, progress, congratulation, gratitude, congregation, inherent, impel, incense, irate, itinerary, transition, transit, inject, projectile, jocular, prejudice, junction, juncture

Word Definitions

gradual **adj.** taking place in stages, or slowly, over an extended period
"There has been a gradual decline in the number of patrons at our restaurant over the past three years."
gradus step, position

graduate **v.** to successfully complete a degree, course, or school; to mark with measurements
"An American yardstick is graduated by one sixteenth-inch lines."
n. a person who has been awarded an academic degree or high school diploma
"George W. Bush is a graduate of Phillips Academy, Andover."
graduation (n.)
graduare to take a degree < *gradus* step, position

ingredient n. any of the foods or substances that are combined to make a particular dish; a component or element
"Inspiration, hard work, and a little luck are the basic ingredients of success."
ingredi to enter: *in-* into + *gradi* to take steps, to advance

progress n. forward or onward movement toward a destination; development toward a better, more complete, or more modern condition
"We've made progress; we are only a few miles from our destination."
v. to move or develop toward a destination, goal, or better condition
"Thomas Edison never progressed beyond grade school."
progression (n.)
progressus advanced; progressed (past participle of *progredi* to come forth; to make progress: *pro-* forward + *gradi* to take steps; to advance)

congratulation(s) n. praise or good wishes on a special occasion
"By way of congratulation, Mr. Smith bought his son a car."
congratulatory (adj.), congratulate (v.)
congratulatio congratulations: *con-* together + *gratulatio* rejoicing; thankful < *gratus* pleasing

gratitude n. appreciation of kindness; thankfulness
"The woman expressed gratitude to the firefighters who saved her kitten."
gratus pleasing, thankful

congregation n. a gathering of people or things; a group of people assembled for religious worship
"A congregation of crows blackened the crown of the tree."
congregate (v.)
congregare to collect (into a flock): *con-* together + *gregare* to gather < *grex, gregis* flock; herd

inherent adj. existing in something as a permanent or essential attribute
"Flowers have inherent beauty, because they are designed to attract the insects or animals they depend on for reproduction."
inhaerere to cling to: *in-* in, upon + *haerere* to stick

impel v. to drive or push toward; to persuade
"The terrorist attacks of Sept. 11, 2001 impelled him to join the Army."
impellere to drive; to push: *im-* in + *pellere* to push

incense v. to make very angry; to infuriate
"Her husband's flirtatious behavior incensed her."
n. a gum, spice, or other substance that is burned for the sweet smell it produces
"The Wise Men brought gold and two precious incenses: frankincense and myrrh."
incendere to set fire to; to provoke or excite

irate adj. extremely angry
"The irate customer dashed off a furious letter to the company."
ira anger, resentment

itinerary n. a planned route of travel or journey
"My European itinerary includes Paris, Geneva, and Barcelona."
iter, itiner journey, road

transition n. the process or period of changing from one condition to another
"The Civil War marked the transition from a primarily agricultural economy to a more industrial one."
transire to go across: *trans-* across + *itum* gone, moved (past participle of the verb *ire*)

transit n. the carrying of people or things from one place to another; an act of passing through or across a place
"Forms of mass transit include trains, buses, subways, and airplanes."
transire to go across: *trans-* across + *itum* gone, moved (past participle of the verb *ire*)

inject v. to force liquid into; to give a shot; to insert in the midst of something
"The porter in *Macbeth* injects a note of humor into an otherwise gloomy drama."
injection (n.)
inicere to throw in: *in-* into + *iacere/jacere* to throw

projectile n. an object that can be thrown; a missile
"David's stone projectile struck Goliath in the temple and slew him."
proicere to throw forth: *pro-* forth + *iacere/jacere* to throw

jocular adj. characterized by joking or wit
"Falstaff is Shakespeare's most famous jocular character."
iocus/jocus joke; game; sport

prejudice n. a preconceived preference or idea formed without reason or experience; a biased opinion
"He bought only French wines, showing a snobbish prejudice against California wines of equal quality."
praejudicium precedent; prejudgment: *prae-* in advance + *judicum* judgment

junction n. the act or process of joining; a place where two roads, railroad lines, or
other things join
"Meet me at the junction of 7th Avenue and 107th Street."
junctus connected; adjoined (past participle of *jungere* to join)

juncture n. a point in time; a turning point or crisis; a joint or junction
"It's now five o'clock. At this juncture, we will recess until nine tomorrow morning."
junctus connected; adjoined (past participle of *jungere* to join)

Exercise A
Use the word box at the beginning of the lesson to fill in the blanks below:

1. While some Episcopal _____ and ministers support the blessing of same-sex unions, others do not, which has caused a deep division within the church.

2. According to the map, the exit is at the _____ of Route 1 and Interstate 95.

3. Her _____ kindness and generosity helped her make new friends with ease.

4. The elderly lady's face glowed with _____ when the Boy Scout offered to carry her groceries.

5. _____ by white Americans toward racial and ethnic minorities has decreased significantly since the early 20th century.

6. The family's summer vacation _____ includes Cleveland, Chicago, and Michigan.

7. The day we _____ from high school was the happiest in our lives.

8. The most important _____ in steak au poivre is steak.

9. The doctor may _____ you with a contrast dye before your CT scan, because the resulting images are much clearer and easier to read.

10. At that _____, he saw there was no point in further argument; her mind was made up.

11. The prisoner became _____ when the one of the guards accused him of going to the infirmary under false pretenses.

12. The wise men gave frankincense and myrrh to the infant Jesus, which is why _____ is still used in formal church services.

13. We made excellent _____ on our trip from San Francisco to Chicago, traveling more than 500 miles each day.

14. The school did not allow _____ in the classroom; however, it did sponsor a paper airplane contest outside on the playground.

15. His brother's assassination _____ Robert Kennedy to run for president.

16. His students made the _____ from high school to college easily, because he prepared them so well.

17. The "T" subway in Boston is a popular form of mass _____.

83

18. Jesters were known as _____ entertainers who performed tricks for – and even poked fun at – kings and their courtiers.

19. The terraces the Incas carved into the mountainside formed a _____ staircase leading to the lofty peak.

20. The New England Patriots were thrilled to receive personal _____ from President Bush for winning the Super Bowl.

Exercise B

Match the word with the letter of its definition:

1. ____ congratulation
2. ____ congregation
3. ____ impel
4. ____ gradual
5. ____ graduate
6. ____ gratitude
7. ____ ingredient
8. ____ inherent
9. ____ incense
10. ____ inject
11. ____ irate
12. ____ itinerary
13. ____ jocular
14. ____ junction
15. ____ juncture
16. ____ prejudice
17. ____ progress
18. ____ projectile
19. ____ transit
20. ____ transition

a) a critical point in time
b) to drive toward
c) extremely angry
d) to infuriate
e) the process of changing
f) a planned route
g) taking place in stages over a period of time
h) acknowledgement and approval
i) a preconceived idea or bias
j) the act of passing from one place to another
k) a component
l) to complete a diploma or degree
m) a gathering of people; a religious flock
n) thankfulness
o) to force liquid into something
p) permanent or essential (of a characteristic or attribute)
q) to move forward
r) humorous
s) a missile; something propelled with force
t) an intersection of two roads or rail lines

Exercise C

ACROSS

2 To give a shot to

4	Taking place in stages, or slowly, over an extended period
6	To make very angry; a substance burned for its scent
7	Extremely angry
9	Forward or onward movement toward a goal
10	Permanent or essential (of an attribute)
13	Appreciation of kindness; thankfulness
16	A place where two roads or train tracks join
18	To successfully complete a degree, course, or school
19	Praise or good wishes on a special occasion

DOWN

1	A critical point in time; a turning point or crisis
3	Characterized by joking or wit
5	The carrying of people or things from one place to another
6	A planned route of travel or journey
8	A preconceived preference or idea; a biased opinion
11	A gathering of people or things
12	One of several foods or substances combined to make a particular dish
14	The process of changing from one condition to another
15	An object that can be thrown; a missile
17	To persuade; to push toward

Lesson XIV

LABOR-, LATERAL, LAV-, LEGIS, LEVIS, LIBER, LICENCIA,
LIGO, LINGUA, LITTERA, LOCUS, LOQU-, LUCIS, LUD-

LABOR-	**LATERAL**	**LAV-**	**LEGIS**	**LEVIS**	**LIBER**	**LICENCIA**
to work	side	to wash	law	light	free	freedom

LIGO	**LINGUA**	**LITTERA**	**LOCUS**	**LOQU-, LOCUT-**	**LUCIS**	**LUD-**
bind	tongue, speech	letter	place	to talk	light	to play

> *laborious, collateral, deluge, legitimate, legacy, delegate, levity,
> liberal, liberty, license, league, lingual, literal, locality,
> eloquent, colloquial, illuminate, lucid, delusion, elusive*

Word Definitions

laborious   **adj.** requiring considerable time and effort
"Digging the 100-foot ditch was laborious."
labor (n.)
laborare to labor, to work < *labor, laboris* labor

collateral   **adj.** situated or running side by side; parallel
"The bomb not only destroyed the military target, but caused a dozen civilian deaths, which the Army euphemistically called 'collateral damage.'"
n. something pledged as security for repayment of a loan; additional but subordinate
"The man gave his Rolex watch as collateral for the $500 loan."
collateralis collateral: *con-* together + *latus, lateris* side

deluge **v.** to overrun with water; to inundate
"The president was deluged with angry e-mails after the preemptive attack."
n. a flood; a drenching downpour of rain
"The deluge after the earthquake multiplied the damage."
diluere to wash away: *de-* down, away from + *luere* to wash
(also *lavare* to wash)

legitimate **adj.** conforming to the law or to the rules; defensible with logic or justification; (of a child) born to a married couple
"The eldest son born to the king and queen is the legitimate heir to the throne."
legitimare to make legal < *legalis* legal, of the law

legacy **n.** an amount of money or property left to someone in a will; something intangible that has been bequeathed or inherited
"His father's reputation as a ne'er-do-well was an unwanted legacy that hindered his own career."
legare to bequeath (under the law) < *lex, legis* law

delegate **n.** a person sent or authorized to represent others; a member of a committee
"The U.S. sent the vice president as a delegate to the international climate summit."
v. to entrust to another person, typically one who is less senior than oneself
"If the boss did not delegate tasks, nothing would be completed on time."
delegare: *de-* down + *legare* to depute

levity **n.** the treatment of a serious matter with humor or lack of respect
"Making jokes at his friend's expense was unpardonable levity."
levis light (in weight)

liberal **adj.** having or giving freely; respectful and accepting of behavior or opinions different from one's own; ample
"The homeowner spread liberal amounts of fertilizer to assure a thick lawn."
liber free

liberty **n.** freedom; the state of being free from oppression or imprisonment; (pl.) overly free or unrestricted actions
"The father warned the young man not to take any liberties with his underage daughter."
libertas freedom; ex-slave; outspokenness < *liber* free

license **n.** 1) a permit from an authority to own or use something, do a particular thing, or carry on a trade; formal or official permission
"Many teenagers are excited to get a driver's license."
n. 2) deviation from normal rules
"A poet will often take license with standard English usage to better express himself."
v. to issue a license; to give someone formal permission to do something
"James Bond was licensed to kill by the British government."
licentiare to authorize; to permit < *licentia* free; unrestrained

league **n.** a union of persons with common aims; a collection of people, countries, or groups that combine for mutual protection or cooperation
"The buccaneers were in league with Andrew Jackson at the Battle of New

Orleans."
ligare to bind or tie

lingual   **adj.** relating to or near the tongue; relating to speech or language
"He grew up in a multi-lingual household; his parents spoke Spanish, English, and Russian."
lingua tongue; language; speech

literal   **adj.** straightforward, not figurative; taking words in their concrete or usual sense; representing the exact words of the original text
"The literal meaning of 'star' is a heavenly body; the figurative meaning refers to a famous person."
littera letter; something written

locality   **n.** a particular neighborhood, place, or district; a specific place
"It was in this locality that the series of brutal muggings took place."
localis local < *locus* place

eloquent   **adj.** forceful and expressive; fluent and expressive (speech)
"The rows of graves in Arlington are eloquent testimony to American war sacrifices."
eloquence (n.)
eloqui to speak out: *ex-* out + *loqui* to speak

colloquial   **adj.** conversational or informal speech or writing (not formal or literary)
"'Colloquial' describes everyday spoken English as opposed to formal, written English."
colloquium conversation: *co-* together + *loqui* to speak

illuminate   **v.** to light up; to make bright; to shed light on a subject
"Hundreds of Japanese lanterns illuminate the tiny cottages at the Oak Bluffs campground once a year on 'Illumination Night.'"
illumination (n.)
illuminatus lit up: *in-* (expressing intensification) + *luminatus* brightened (past participle of the verb *lumare*, to brighten) < *lumen, luminis* light; lamp; daylight

lucid   **adj.** easy to follow; clear
"As the general anesthesia wears off, it may take a while for the patient to become lucid again."
lucere to shine < *lux, lucis* light; day; life

delusion   **n.** an idiosyncratic belief or impression that is not in accordance with generally accepted reality; an incorrect idea or belief
"Hitler's belief that Germany could quickly conquer England proved to be a delusion."
delude (v.)
deludere to deceive; to play false: *de-* away from + *ludere* to play

elusive   **adj.** difficult to find, catch, or achieve
"Despite his determination, straight As proved an elusive goal."
eludere to elude: *ex-* out, away + *ludere* to play

Exercise A

Use the word box at the beginning of the lesson to fill in the blanks below:

1. The graduation speaker was so _____ that the students and faculty gave her a standing ovation.

2. Major _____ Baseball employs only the best baseball players in the country.

3. After Michelle Obama did an in-depth radio interview, there was a _____ of phone calls from listeners.

4. Julia Child often added a _____ quantity of wine to her sauces and entrées.

5. According to the local court, the homeowner had a _____ claim to the piece of land in dispute.

6. Even though most of the movie was filmed on the set in Hollywood, the director cut in street scenes from Charlestown to establish the film's fictional _____.

7. She went to the Democratic National Convention as a _____ for John Edwards, but ended up voting for Barack Obama.

8. His only _____ to his children was a small investment portfolio.

9. The bank accepted the property as _____ to secure the new business loan.

10. "Get the lead out" is a _____ expression for "Please, move faster!"

11. The moderator was expert at using _____ to keep the audience's attention focused.

12. "Give me _____ or give me death" is a famous quotation attributed to Patrick Henry at the time of the Revolutionary War.

13. Every set of new parents operates under the _____ that their baby is the cutest in the entire world.

14. The _____ area was very sore, so the patient had to "eat" a liquid diet through a straw.

15. Those who suffer from autism spectrum disorders often have difficulty understanding humor based on wordplay, as their minds are very _____.

16. Strategically placed solar lights will _____ the borders of the driveway at night.

17. Because restaurant work is so _____ and low-paid, the burnout rate is high for people who work in the kitchens.

89

18. We could hear the spring peepers all around us, but when we tried to spot them, they proved _____.

19. The robbers were under the false impression that an "open door policy" gave them a _____ to steal.

20. Her thinking and speech were _____ until she suffered a second stroke.

Exercise B
Match the word with the letter of its definition:

1. ____ collateral
2. ____ colloquial
3. ____ delegate
4. ____ delusion
5. ____ deluge
6. ____ eloquent
7. ____ elusive
8. ____ illuminate
9. ____ laborious
10. ____ legitimate
11. ____ levity
12. ____ league
13. ____ legacy
14. ____ liberal
15. ____ liberty
16. ____ license
17. ____ lingual
18. ____ literal
19. ____ locality
20. ____ lucid

a) articulate and expressive
b) freedom
c) something bequeathed at death
d) familiar and conversational
e) to shed light on
f) lighthearted or humorous speech
g) relating to the tongue
h) an area or specific site
i) requiring considerable time and effort
j) to entrust to someone
k) something pledged as security for a loan
l) having or giving freely
m) straightforward; using the exact words
n) conforming to the law
o) clear
p) an unrealistic idea or belief
q) to flood or inundate
r) difficult to find or achieve
s) a union of persons or countries
t) a permit or official permission

Exercise C

ACROSS
1 An amount of money or property left to someone in a will
3 Respectful of behavior or beliefs different from one's own; generous
4 Requiring considerable time and effort

5 A union of persons with common aims
6 To light up; to make bright
7 Something pledged as security for repayment of a loan
12 An unrealistic idea or belief
15 Straightforward, not figurative; taking words in their concrete sense
16 A particular neighborhood, place, or district
17 Relating to or near the tongue; relating to speech or language
18 A person sent or authorized to represent others

DOWN
2 Conversational or informal speech or writing

3 A permit from an authority to own or use something
5 The treatment of a serious matter with humor or lack of due respect
8 Conforming to the law or to the rules
9 Difficult to find, catch, or achieve
10 Freedom; the state of being free from oppression or imprisonment
11 A drenching rainstorm; a flood
13 Forceful and expressive
14 Easy to follow; clear

Lesson XV

MANUS, MAR, MATER, MEDIUS, MEM-,
MENDUM, MERG-, MINUS, MISS-, MOT–

| *MANUS* hand | *MAR* sea | *MATER, MATR-* mother | *MEDIUS* middle | *MEM-* to remember |

| *MENDUM* defect, fault | *MERG-, MERS-* dip, plunge | *MINUS* less | *MISS-* to send | *MOT-, MOV-* to move |

mandatory, manipulate, manufacture, maritime, maternal, matrimony, medieval, mediocre, memorabilia, memory, mend, immersion, merge, minimal, minimize, missile, moment, momentum, motion, promise

Word Definitions

mandatory **adj.** required by law, rule, or other obligation
"Military service was mandatory for all Spartan males from the age of 8."
mandare to order; to give in hand; to entrust: *manus* hand + *dare* to give

manipulate **v.** to handle or control with dexterity; to control or influence; to change to serve one's own ends
"Dictators typically manipulate vote-counting to guarantee their reelection."
maniple a handful; a company of soldiers < *manus* hand

manufacture **v.** to make or process into a finished product; to fabricate
"The tardy student's excuse of a flat tire was manufactured."
manus hand + *facere* to make

maritime **adj.** of, relating to, or along the sea
"The Canadian Maritimes is the name given to those provinces bordering the Atlantic Ocean."

maritimus of or near the sea; coastal < *mare, maris* sea

maternal   **adj.** related through one's mother; concerning motherhood
"My mother's sisters and brothers are my maternal aunts and uncles."
mater mother

matrimony   **n.** the rites of marriage; the state of being married
"Holy matrimony is a sacred rite in the Roman Catholic Church."
matrimonius matrimony, marriage < *mater* mother

medieval   **adj.** belonging to or having to do with the Middle Ages; antiquated or outdated
"Some countries continue to use medieval punishments, such as amputation of a hand for theft."
medius middle

mediocre   **adj.** of average to inferior quality
"The middle school students' mediocre performance on the standardized tests lowered the entire school district's ranking."
mediocrity (n.)
medius middle

memorabilia   **n.** objects kept or collected because of their associations with memorable people or events
"Souvenirs are often memorabilia of places we have visited."
memorabilis memorable < *memoria, memoriae* memory

memory   **n.** the mental faculty of retaining and recalling past experience
"'Memory' is the capacity of men or machines to embed and later retrieve information."
memorize (v.)
memoria, memoriae memory

mend   **v.** to fix something broken or torn; to restore to good condition
"'Mending fences' means to make up for past disputes and become friendly again."
mendum, mendi defect; fault

immersion   **n.** the act of covering completely in liquid; complete absorption in a situation or subject
"The Army uses the immersion method to teach languages."
immergere to dip into: *in-* into + *mergere* to plunge

merge   **v.** to combine or be combined into a single entity
"One of the most difficult tasks for new drivers is learning to merge onto an interstate."
mergere to plunge, to immerse

minimal   **adj.** the least amount; of the smallest amount, quantity, or degree
"Even a minimal amount of gluten in her food can make her deathly ill."
minimus small, little

minimize   **v.** to reduce to the least or smallest size

"A flu shot should minimize your chances of coming down with the disease."
minimus small, little

missile   **n.** an object that is fired, thrown, dropped, or otherwise projected at a target; a projectile
"There is an international ban on intercontinental ballistic missiles, or ICBMs."
missile, missiles missile < *missus* thrown; sent (past participle of *mittere* to send; to throw)

promise   **n.** a written or spoken statement binding a person to an action
"I promise to tell the truth, the whole truth, and nothing but the truth."
promittere to put forth, to promise: *pro-* before + *mittere* to send

moment   **n.** a very brief period of time; importance or consequence; a particular time (in history)
"For a moment, I thought the woman was my dead aunt, but I realized immediately that she couldn't be."
momentum moment; movement < *motus* movement

momentum   **n.** the impetus gained by a moving object
"Trains build great momentum and cannot stop quickly"
momentum moment; movement < *motus* movement

motion   **n.** the action or process of moving
"The ball was in motion while it was rolling down the hill."
motus movement (past participle of *movere* to move)

Exercise A

Use the word box at the beginning of the lesson to fill in the blanks below:

1. The toy company tried, but failed, to _____ enough action figures to meet holiday demand.

2. Jesus was baptized by _____ in the Jordan River.

3. In comparison to Krispy Kreme doughnuts, Dunkin' Donuts treats are only _____.

4. A person used to public speaking can prepare a speech with _____ notice, but I need at least a week.

5. In _____ times, there was a strict social caste system with little opportunity for upward mobility.

6. The _____ of the roller-coaster left him nauseated and dizzy.

7. He made a solemn _____ at his swearing-in to uphold the U.S. Constitution.

8. The business executives _____ the accounts to show greater sales revenues than they actually had, artificially driving up the stock's share price.

9. Sports fanatics often collect _____ of their favorite teams.

10. _____ can be a big adjustment for older newlyweds who have been used to living on their own.

11. "To take a trip down _____ lane" is to indulge in pleasant or sentimental memories.

12. After much deliberation, the two local banks decided to _____ so as to withstand competition from larger, regional banks.

13. The little girl was devoted to her _____ grandmother, who often took care of her when her mother had to work late.

14. Once the _____ is airborne, it is monitored by NASA with instruments on the ground.

15. The _____ came when he needed to act decisively or risk losing her.

16. At most liberal arts colleges, writing courses are _____ , but at others they are optional.

17. Many New England states sponsor a _____ academy to train those who wish to join the Coast Guard or make their living on the sea.

18. I told him to _____ his ways, or I would fire him.

19. The _____ of the sled carried him into the tree before he had time to correct course.

20. Botox injections can _____ wrinkles by paralyzing the tiny muscles that cause them.

Exercise B
Match the word with the letter of its definition:

1. ____ immersion
2. ____ manipulate
3. ____ mandatory
4. ____ manufacture
5. ____ maritime
6. ____ maternal
7. ____ matrimony
8. ____ medieval
9. ____ mediocre
10. ____ memorabilia

a) a projectile
b) related through one's mother
c) the action or process of moving
d) the mental faculty of retaining information
e) belonging to the Middle Ages
f) to cleverly control or influence, especially for one's own benefit
g) the least possible
h) to combine into a single entity
i) of average quality
j) covering completely with liquid

11. ____ **memory**   k) a very brief period of time
12.
13.
14.
15.
16.
17.
18.
19.
20.

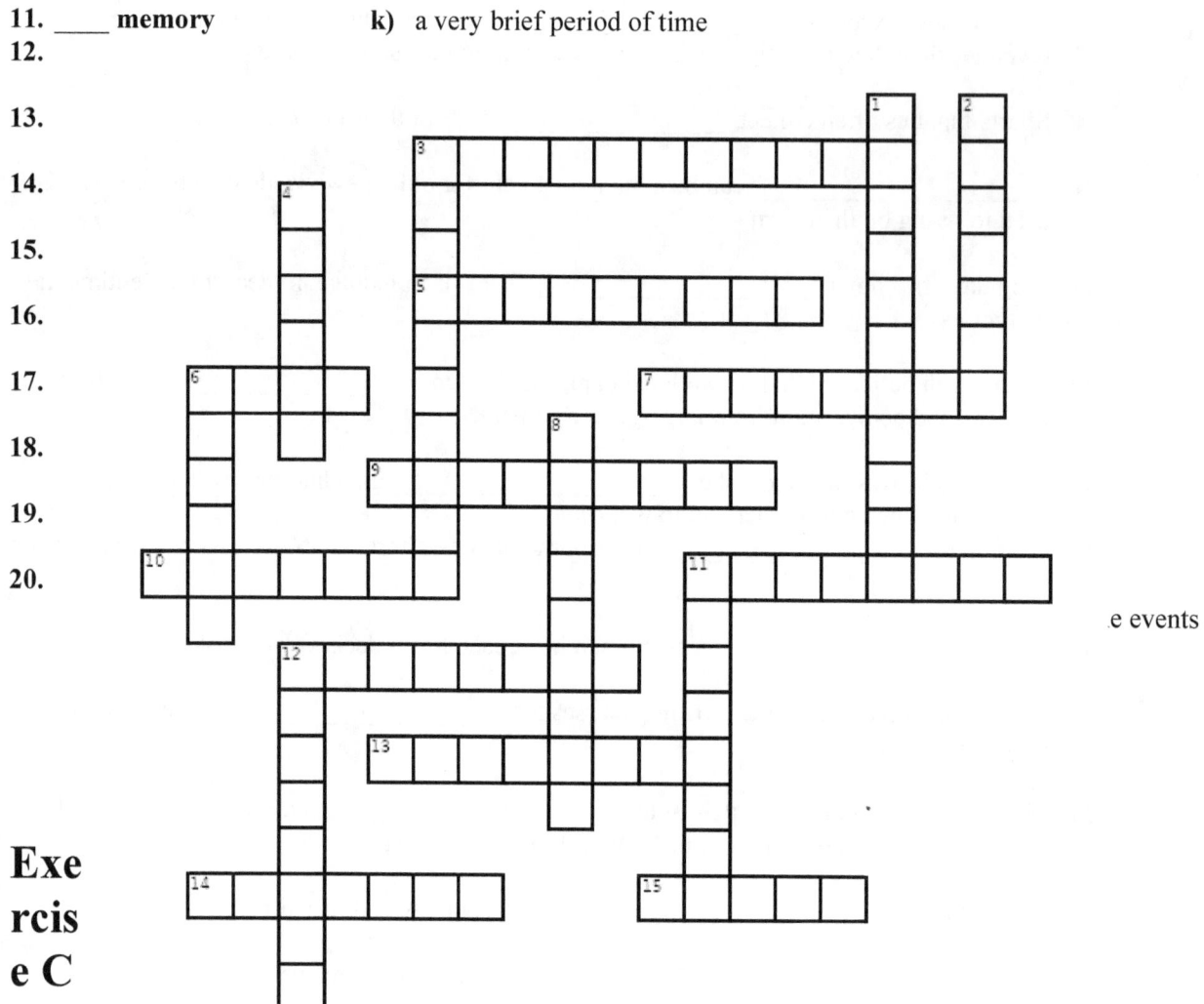

...e events

Exercise C

ACROSS
3 Objects kept because of their associations with memorable people or events
5 The act of covering completely with a liquid
6 To fix
7 Of average or inferior quality
9 Required by law, rule, or other obligation

10 A written or spoken statement binding a person to an action
11 Antiquated; outdated
12 Of, relating to, or along the sea
13 The impetus gained by a moving object
14 The least amount; of the smallest amount, quantity, or degree
15 To combine or to be combined into a single entity

3   To handle or control with dexterity
4   A very brief period of time
6   The mental faculty of retaining and recalling past experiences
8   The rites of marriage; the state of being married
11 To reduce to the least or smallest size
12 Related through one's mother

DOWN
1 To make or process into a finished product, to fabricate
2 An object that is fired, thrown, or dropped

Quiz 3

> transition, dormant, genuine, levity, fragment, immersion, fragile, legacy, congregation, progress, lucid, irate, fortunate, elusive, mediocre, liberal, deface, fertile, mandatory, incense

1. The _____ from high school to college often causes much anxiety for students and parents alike.

2. My mother became _____ after the store manager refused to let her return the defective towels.

3. The teacher left a rich intellectual _____, but her children didn't inherit much money.

4. The vase was quite _____, and she was _____ that it did not break when she dropped it.

5. Although the Nile River Valley remains _____, many of its ancient tombs have been _____ by grave robbers seeking archaeological treasures.

6. When the window shattered, a _____ of glass struck his eye.

7. Harold Bloom's lectures were filled with obscure references, but his teaching assistant gave _____ explanations afterward to the confused undergraduates.

8. While I was in the hospital, my friend tried to cheer me up with _____, but I knew that underneath his humorous facade, he felt _____ concern.

9. At some colleges, mastery of a foreign language is _____; as a result, many students travel abroad for language _____ programs.

10. The labor union and management negotiators made some _____ on minor issues, but an agreement on wages and benefits remained _____.

11. Despite the student's powerful intellect, his essay was disappointingly _____.

12. Antigua, Guatemala is surrounded by three _____ volcanoes.

13. The _____ bowed their heads in prayer as the priest processed down the aisle, swinging a censer filled with burning _____.

14. A supporter of gay marriage and abortion rights, he was much more _____ than his sister, a Catholic and staunch Republican.

Lesson XVI

MON-, MONS, MOR-, MORI, MUT-, NAT-, NAVIS,
NEG-, NIHIL, NOMEN, NOV-, NOCT, NUNCI-

MON-	*MONS, MONTIS*	*MOR-, MOS-*	*MORI, MORT-*	*MUT-*	*NAT-*
to warn	mountain	custom	to die	to change	born

NAVIS	*NEG-*	*NIHIL*	*NOMEN*	*NOV-*	*NOCT-*	*NUNCI-*
ship	to deny	nothing	name	new	night	to announce

> *monitor, muster, mountain, morality, immortal, mortify, commute, mutate, native, naval, navigate, negate, negative, annihilate, nominal, innovation, novelty, novice, nocturnal, announce*

Word Definitions

monitor
v. to observe and check over a period of time
"Teachers are required to monitor their students' academic progress."
n. a person or device that watches over something
"Andy used a baby monitor so he'd hear when his son woke from his nap."
monitorial (adj.)
monere to warn; to advise

muster
v. to gather together; to collect; to summon for military service
"A sip of wine may aid in mustering the courage to go on stage and speak."
monstrare to show < *monstrum* sign < *monere* to warn; to advise

mountain
n. a conical elevation of the earth's surface, rising to a summit
"One of my favorite pastimes is mountain climbing."

mons, montis mountain

morality **n.** a set of principles of conduct; a system of ideas of right and wrong
"In response to the Civil Rights Movement, some Southerners argued that morality could not be legislated."
moralis concerning philosophy or ethics < *mos, moris* custom; behavior; morals

immortal **adj.** living forever; unable to die; deathless
"'Ozymandias' is a Keats' poem reminding that even a pharaoh is not immortal."
immortality (n.)
immortalis everlasting: *im-* not + *mortalis* mortal; transient; human

mortify **v.** to humiliate or embarrass
"Nude beaches still mortify most Americans; Europeans are much more accepting of public nudity."
mortification (n.)
mortificare to kill; to subdue to weakness < *mors, mortis* death + *ficare* to make; to do (variant of *facere*)

commute **v.** to go from one place to another; to travel the distance between one's home and place of work on a regular basis; to substitute or to exchange
"The murderer's death sentence was commuted by the governor to life without parole."
commuter (n.)
commutare: com- together; including + *mutare* to change

mutate **v.** to undergo or cause to undergo mutation (change or alteration)
"Alchemists sought a Philosopher's Stone to mutate common metals into gold."
mutare to change

native **adj.** existing in or belonging to by nature
"Tomatoes, potatoes, cocoa, and tobacco are native to the Americas."
n. one born in or connected with a place of birth; an original inhabitant of a place; aborigine
"Michael Jordan is a native of Brooklyn, where he learned to play basketball at an early age."
nasci to be born; to grow < *natus* son; child

naval **adj.** relating to ships or shipping; relating to a navy
"Land-locked Switzerland is not a naval power."
navis ship

navigate **v.** to plan or direct the route or course of a ship, airplane, etc; to sail or travel; to find one's way
"Strangers have difficulty navigating Boston's winding and often unmarked streets."

navigare to sail: *navis* ship + *agere* to drive

negate
v. to make ineffective or invalid; to nullify; to deny the existence of
"The apparent goal was negated by the referee's offsides call."
negare to deny

negative
n. a statement or act indicating or expressing a contradiction, denial, or refusal; describing a number less than zero; exposed film, in which the colors (or black and white) are inverted
"In radio transmissions, military personnel and airline pilots say 'Negative' instead of 'No.'"

adj. the absence of something
"There is much negative space in an atom."
negativity (n.), negation (n.)
negatio, negationis denial; refusal < *negare* to deny

annihilate
v. to destroy completely
"The Romans annihilated Carthage, razing the city and plowing salt into its fields."
annihilation (n.), annihilator (n.)
annihilare to reduce to nothing: *ad-* to + *nihil* nothing

nominal
adj. existing in name only; very small; far below real value or cost
"'To get it for a song' means to pay a nominal price for a thing."
nomen name

innovation
n. the act of beginning or introducing something for the first time
"The transistor was the crucial innovation that led to microchip technology."
innovare to renew: *in-* into + *novere* to make new

novelty
n. something new and unusual; the quality of being novel
"The automobile was a novelty until mass production and extensive paved roads brought down the price and made it practical to use."
novel (adj.)
novus new

novice
n. someone who is beginning; a person who is new to and inexperienced in a job or situation; a rookie
"When he was a novice at golf, he had a high handicap, but it quickly dropped after he took lessons."
novus new

nocturnal
adj. occurring or active at night
"Owls and bats are nocturnal creatures: They hunt at night and sleep during the day."
nocturnus of the night < *nox, noctis* night

announce
v. to make known publicly
"'The Wedding March' traditionally announces that the bride is starting down the aisle."
announcement (n.)

annuntiare to announce < *nuncio* messenger; herald; message

Exercise A

Use the word box at the beginning of the lesson to fill in the blanks below:

1. _____ people inhabited North America at least 10,000 to 12,000 years ago.

2. In Greek mythology, the _____ gods live on Mount Olympus.

3. To make "a _____ out of a molehill" is an expression meaning to exaggerate something or to make a huge fuss over a minor problem.

4. The _____ of the printing press made books available and affordable beyond the aristocracy and religious orders.

5. He decided to _____ his former girlfriend by posting embarrassing photos of her on Facebook.

6. She used to spend two or more hours each day on her _____ into the city.

7. In 1492, Christopher Columbus _____ across the Atlantic ocean to the New World, thinking he was going to India.

8. Animals that are more active at night than during the day are _____.

9. At first, Powerpoint presentations were a _____, but now few people dare to lecture without one.

10. The anchors will _____ the Powerball lottery winner on the evening news.

11. In Robert Louis Stevenson's famous novel about a man with a split personality, the amiable and moral Dr. Jekyll _____ into his brutish and misanthropic alter-ego, Mr. Hyde.

12. The Minutemen _____ on the town green in Lexington to confront the Redcoats.

13. Although he invested steadily in his retirement plan, a sudden decline in the stock market threatened to _____ most of his gains.

14. During the Crusades, it was not unusual for one force to _____ another on the battlefield.

15. A special device linked to the thermostat will _____ the temperature and humidity inside the library, and sound an alarm if they sink too low.

16. _____ as well as land battles were fought in the Revolutionary War, as England was a major maritime power.

17. A _____ sales tax increase of ¼ percent allowed Arkansas to better fund its fish and wildlife agency.

18. The mother's _____ comments hurt her sensitive son's feelings.

19. The _____ of the times allowed the English to capture Native Americans to act as guides in New England.

20. At the ski resort, my friends and I will stick to the _____ trails until we get more practice.

Exercise B

Match the word with the letter of its definition:

1. ____ annihilate
2. ____ announce
3. ____ commute
4. ____ immortal
5. ____ innovation
6. ____ monitor
7. ____ morality
8. ____ mortify
9. ____ mountain
10. ____ muster
11. ____ mutate
12. ____ naval
13. ____ native
14. ____ navigate
15. ____ negate
16. ____ negative
17. ____ nocturnal
18. ____ nominal
19. ____ novelty
20. ____ novice

a) active at night
b) to travel a certain distance regularly
c) something new and/or unusual
d) to make known publically
e) a set of principles of conduct
f) to undergo a change or alteration
g) relating to ships
h) a conical, natural elevation of the earth's surface
i) to invalidate
j) original to a particular person or place
k) to destroy completely
l) an inexperienced person
m) to humiliate
n) a contradiction, denial, or refusal
o) to gather together
p) a new method, idea, or product
q) symbolic or minimal; existing in name only
r) to travel on a desired course
s) living forever
t) to observe over time

Exercise C

ACROSS
1. To make ineffective or invalid; to nullify
3. To gather together; to collect
4. To humiliate or embarrass
6. A tall, natural feature of the earth's surface
8. Something new and unusual; the quality of being very novel
10. Unable to die
12. To proclaim publicly
15. Occurring or active at night
16. Existing in or belonging to by nature
17. To destroy completely

DOWN
1. Existing in name only; very small; far below real value or cost
2. Tending to contradict, deny, or refuse
5. To go from one place to another regularly
6. A set of principles of ethical conduct
7. To plan and direct the route or course of a ship
9. Someone who is beginning; a person who is new to the job
10. The act of introducing something for the first time
11. To observe and check over a period of time
13. To undergo a change or alteration
14. Relating to ships or shipping; relating to a navy

Lesson XVII

OCULUS, ODI-, OLE-, OPER-, ORA-, ORBIS, ORDO, ORN-, OSTEND-, PASC-, PASS-, PATER, PAX, PECCATUM, PECUNIA, PEL-, PEND-, PED

OCULUS	ODI-	OLE-	OPER-	ORA-	ORBIS
eye	to hate	to smell	to work	to speak, pray	circle; sphere

ORDO	ORN-	OSTEND-	PASC-	PASS-	PATER
order	to decórate, adorn	to exhibit	to feed	to feel, suffer	father

PAX	PECCATUM	PECUNIA	PEL-, PULS-	PEND-	PED
peace	sin	money	to drive	to hang; weigh	foot

> *oculist, odious, olfactory, operate, orator, orbit, ordain, ornate, ostentatious, repast, passionate, patriotism, patron, pacify, impeccable, pecuniary, propeller, pendant, pedestrian, pedal*

World Definitions

oculist   n. a person who treats diseases or defects of the eye
"Ben Franklin proved himself an amateur oculist with his invention of bifocals."
oculus eye

odious **adj.** extremely unpleasant; repulsive; hateful
"Cleaning a septic tank is an odious task, even to professionals."
odiousness (n.)
odium hatred

olfactory **adj.** relating to the sense of smell
"Most of the sense of taste in fact derives from the olfactory organ: the nose."
olfacere to smell

operate **v.** to function or control the function of; to manage or run
"Mob bosses stereotypically operate out of pizza parlors and bars."
operator (n.)
operare to work < *opus, operis* need; work

orator **n.** a public speaker, especially one who is proficient
"With his masterful speech, orator Daniel Webster overwhelmed the Devil."
orate (v.), oration (n.)
orator speaker < *orare* to pray

orbit **n.** the regular elliptical course of a smaller celestial object around a larger one; the network of people who come into contact with a person or family; proximity
"Wealthy families rarely admit the financially inferior into their social orbit."
v. to revolve around (literally or figuratively)
"Earth orbits the Sun once every year."
orbitus circular < *orbis* circle; sphere

ordain **v.** to confer holy orders upon; to order or appoint officially
"After years of study in a seminary, a theologian may be ordained as a minister."
ordinare to arrange; to appoint < *ordo, ordinis* row; rank; series

ornament **n.** an object used or serving to decorate something
"A car's hood ornament serves no purpose beyond decoration and branding."
ornare to adorn

ornate **adj.** extremely decorated; elaborately covered; extensively designed
"Notre Dame has many ornate statues and carvings on its exterior."
ornare to adorn

ostentatious **adj.** characterized by pretentious or showy display; designed to impress
"Those from monied families often complain that the nouveaux riches are too ostentatious, announcing their wealth with gaudy jewelry and flashy cars."
ostendere to show; to display < *tendere* to stretch; to spread

repast **n.** a meal
"A roasted, stuffed turkey is the standard centerpiece of the Thanksgiving repast."
re- (expressing intensive force) + *pascere* to feed

passionate	**adj.** having or showing strong feelings; unstinting devotion "Anthony and Cleopatra pursued a passionate love affair before their mutual suicide." *pati* to suffer; to endure; to allow
patriotism	**n.** love of one's country and a willingness to defend it "Americans display their patriotism with parades, and fireworks on July Fourth." *patriot (n.)* *pater, patris* father
patron	**n.** a person who gives financial and other support "Theater patrons are asked to switch off their cell phones during performances." *patronage (n.)* *pater, patris* father
pacify	**v.** to quiet; to bring peace to "Unable to pacify the savage Picts, Hadrian built a wall along the Scottish border." *pacificare* to pacify < *pax, pacis* peace; harmony
impeccable	**adj.** flawless; perfect; in accordance with the highest standards "The credentials of the Supreme Court candidate were impeccable." *im-* not + *peccare* to sin
pecuniary	**adj.** pertaining to money "A pecuniary reward was offered for information leading to the suspect's arrest." *pecunia* money
propeller	**n.** a rotating, fan-like device for driving an aircraft or boat "A jet's turbine engines outperform an airplane's propellers." *propellere* to drive forward: *pro-* forward + *pellere* to drive
pendant	**n.** an ornament suspended from something else, usually a necklace "After she developed arthritis in her hands, she wore her wedding ring as a pendant on a gold chain." *pendere* to hang
pedestrian	**n.** a person traveling by foot; common, ordinary "Even though pedestrians have the right of way at intersections, many drivers believe that might makes right." *pedester* going on foot < *pes, pedis* foot
pedal	**n.** a foot-operated lever "A foot pedal operated the spinning wheel and spinning Jenny." *pes, pedis* foot

Exercise A

Use the word box at the beginning of the lesson to fill in the blanks below:

1. Lorenzo de Medici, a _____ of the arts during the Renaissance, supported Michelangelo and Leonardo da Vinci.

2. Although forklifts look easy to _____, they are frequently involved in workplace accidents because they tip over easily.

3. She gave a bottle to the crying baby to _____ him, and he quickly went to sleep.

4. Gaudy costume jewelry is too _____ for my taste; I prefer simple, delicate earrings and necklaces.

5. The midday _____ was enormous, so afterwards he took a nap.

6. If you are fortunate enough to find a vocation you are _____ about, you will never regret your everyday employment.

7. The bishop prepared to _____ her as a minister, despite the controversy within the church over women clergy.

8. The candidate for student council president had an _____ reputation and was easily elected.

9. Once he enters a crosswalk, a _____ has the right of way.

10. The _____ sense is closely related to the sense of taste; if something smells good, it probably tastes good as well.

11. When bicycling uphill, you need to _____ faster in a lower gear.

12. A patient with pink eye should be checked out by an _____.

13. Students might calculate the _____ of a planet in an astronomy class.

14. The bully's _____ behavior offended the entire school.

15. After the terrorist attacks of Sept. 11, 2001 stalled the economy, President George W. Bush declared that shopping was an act of _____.

16. The valedictorian is typically the student _____ at high school graduation.

17. She was looking for a suitable _____ to put on her antique gold chain.

18. Rococo architecture is characterized by its use of elaborate decorative elements, such as _____ statues and florid, gold-painted moldings.

19. Every year, hundreds of manatees, whales, dolphins, and other marine mammals are fatally injured by boat _____.

20. The hospital had to pay _____ damages and change its policies after the successful malpractice lawsuit.

Exercise B

Match the word with the letter of its definition:

1. ____ impeccable
2. ____ oculist
3. ____ odious
4. ____ olfactory
5. ____ operate
6. ____ orator
7. ____ orbit
8. ____ ordain
9. ____ ornate
10. ____ ostentatious
11. ____ pacify
12. ____ passionate
13. ____ patriotism
14. ____ patron
15. ____ pecuniary
16. ____ pedal
17. ____ pedestrian
18. ____ pendant
19. ____ propeller
20. ____ repast

a) characterized by pretentious display
b) to manage or function
c) the rotation of a smaller heavenly body around a larger one
d) strong support for one's country
e) hateful; extremely unpleasant
f) to make quiet; to bring peace
g) relating to money
h) a foot-operated lever or control
i) a person who gives financial support
j) faultless
k) to appoint officially
l) highly decorated
m) a person travelling by foot
n) one who treats eye diseases
o) having or showing powerful emotions
p) a suspended ornament
q) a meal
r) a proficient public speaker
s) relating to the sense of smell
t) a fan-like device that drives an aircraft or boat

Exercise C

ACROSS
2. Pertaining to money
6. Characterized by pretentious or showy display
7. The love of one's country and the willingness to defend it
8. To function or control the function of; to manage or run
12. A person traveling by foot; common, ordinary
14. A person who gives financial support
16. Detailed and decorative
17. A proficient public speaker

DOWN
1. To confer holy orders on; to order or appoint officially
2. To make quiet; to bring peace to
3. Flawless; perfect
4. A person who treats diseases or defects of the eye
5. Having or showing strong feelings; unstinting in one's devotion
6. Relating to the sense of smell
9. An ornament suspended from something else
10. A foot-operated lever
11. A fan-like device for driving an aircraft or boat forward or backward
13. A meal
15. The regularly repeated elliptical course of a celestial object
16. Extremely unpleasant; repulsive; hateful

Lesson XVIII

PET-, PICTUS, PIUS, PLAC-, PON-, PONDUS, PONS,
PORT-, PORTUS, POTEN-, POT-, PRAEDA, PREHEND-

PET- to seek	*PICTUS* painted	*PIUS, PIET-* duty, dutiful	*PLAC-* to please	
PON- to put; place	*PONDUS* weight	*PONS* bridge	*PORT-* to carry	*PORTUS* port; harbor
POTEN- able; powerful	*POT-* to drink	*PRAEDA* spoils of war	*PREHEND-* to catch	

*appetite, petition, depict, piety, pittance, placid, imposter,
postpone, proponent, ponderous, pontiff, portable, opportune, impotent,,
potential, potable, potion, predatory, apprehend, reprisal*

Word Definitions

appetite   **n.** an instinctive physical desire, especially for food or drink
"The bone-weary soldiers had no appetite for battle that day."
appetize (v.)
appetere to strive after: *ad-* to + *petere* to seek

petition   **n.** a formal request to a superior authority for a right or benefit

"The Magna Carta ensued from the nobles' petition for rights from King John."
petere to seek; to request

depict
v. to represent in a picture or sculpture
"The face of George Washington is depicted on both the quarter and dollar bill."
depiction (n.)
de- completely + *pictus* pictured (past participle of *pingare* to picture)

piety
n. reverence or devotion to God
"A pilgrimage to Mecca is a prescribed act of piety for all Muslims."
pious (adj.)
pius pious; devoted

pittance
n. a small amount of money; the ration in a religious order
"The cost of a meal at McDonald's is a pittance compared to the tab at the Four Seasons."
pietas, pietatis sense of duty; piety

placid
adj. (of water) having an undisturbed appearance; not easily upset or excited; calm
"The Buddha's placid expression is the outward face of inner peace."
placere to calm; to appease

imposter
n. a person who deceives by taking a false identity
"A wolf in sheep's clothing is a familiar metaphor for an imposter."
imponere to inflict; to deceive: *im-* on + *ponere* to put

postpone
v. to put off until later
"He decided to postpone the wedding until he finished his tour in Iraq."
post- after + *ponere* to put

proponent
n. an advocate; an open supporter
"An atomic power proponent, Admiral Rickover lobbied for the nuclear submarine."
proponere to propose; to set forth: *pro-* forth *ponere* to put

ponderous
adj. having great weight; labored and dull
"The windy and dull keynote speaker gave a ponderous speech."
ponderare to weigh < *pondus, ponderis* weight; burden

pontiff
n. the Pope or a bishop
"Pope John Paul II was the first Polish pontiff."
pontifex pontifex < *pons, pont-* bridge + *facere* to build

portable
adj. easily carried or moved
"A picnic involves a portable feast."
portability (n.)
portare to carry

opportune	**adj.** suited or right for a particular purpose; especially convenient or appropriate "Mistletoe provides an opportune excuse to kiss someone." opportunity (n.) *opportunus* suitable; useful; advantageous: *ob-* to + *portus* harbor
impotent	**adj.** weak; helpless; powerless "Samson was rendered impotent when Delilah cut off his hair." impotence (n.) *in-* not + *posse* to be powerful; to be able < *potentia* power
potential	**adj.** having the capacity to develop into something in the future "The threat of a scandal had the potential to derail his candidacy." *potentia* power
potable	**adj.** drinkable "Desalinization makes seawater potable." *potare* to drink
potion	**n.** a liquid with healing, magical, or poisonous powers "Absinthe liqueur contains wood alcohol, making the drink a poisonous potion." *potare* to drink
predatory	**adj.** characterized by plundering; preying naturally on others "Loan sharks charge such predatory interest rates that their dealings are illegal." predator (n.) *praeda* booty; spoils of war
apprehend	**v.** to take into custody; to arrest for a crime; to perceive or understand "Robert E. Lee apprehended John Brown in the Harper's Ferry armory." apprehension (n.) *apprehendere* apprehend: *ad-* towards + *prehendere* to seize; to lay hold of
reprisal	**n.** an act of retaliation "A trade embargo was the U.S. reprisal for Castro's ties to the Soviet Union." *reprehendere* to seize; to check; to rebuke: *re-* again + *prehendere* to seize

Exercise A

Use the word box at the beginning of the lesson to fill in the blanks below:

1. To indicate that the water is restricted to hand-washing only and should not be drunk, a sign over a restroom sink will state "not _____."

2. The _____ pirate lives off the theft of other peoples' goods.

3. "An eye for an eye, a tooth for a tooth" is a Biblical proverb used to justify _____ for wrongs or injuries inflicted on a person or society.

4. The "Pen Hens" decided they would _____ their meeting, as three members could not attend on the scheduled date.

5. The Pacific Ocean was so named because it is relatively _____ compared to the Atlantic.

6. When the wealthy man refused to give the beggar a dollar, a passerby commented that the sum was a mere _____.

7. Da Vinci painted the Mona Lisa to _____ Lisa Gherardini, who was known for her enigmatic smile.

8. When his employer praised the project he had just completed, it seemed to be an _____ moment to ask for a raise.

9. The sheriff was a strong _____ of making handguns illegal.

10. The desperate man went to a witch doctor seeking a love _____, in hopes it would make Anna Maria desire him.

11. His rage was _____: He had no way to avenge himself on the prosecutor, judge, and jury who had convicted him and sentenced him to life in prison.

12. Some of the appliances are _____; the movers can easily disconnect and transport them to your new home.

13. The authorities went to the Japanese airport to _____ Bobby Fisher on charges of violating sanctions against Yugoslavia in 1993.

14. We hope that a less conservative _____ in Rome will be more attuned to our contemporary spiritual needs.

15. When the real estate broker showed the house to _____ buyers, she highlighted its best features.

16. They gathered signatures for a _____ to stop clear-cutting in the national forest.

17. His _____ build and slow gait belied his light wit and lively speech.

18. When Barbara went to the casino to redeem her $5,000 prize, she was greatly surprised to discover that an _____ had already been there and claimed her winning.

19. _____ is required of those who would join a Christian monastic order.

20. Jack's _____ was satisfied when he ate a Quarter Pounder with Biggie Fries.

Exercise B
Match the word with the letter of its definition:

1. ____ **appetite**
2. ____ **apprehend**
3. ____ **depict**
4. ____ **imposter**
5. ____ **impotent**
6. ____ **opportune**
7. ____ **petition**
8. ____ **piety**
9. ____ **pittance**
10. ____ **placid**
11. ____ **ponderous**
12. ____ **pontiff**
13. ____ **portable**
14. ____ **postpone**
15. ____ **potable**
16. ____ **potential**
17. ____ **potion**
18. ____ **predatory**
19. ____ **proponent**
20. ____ **reprisal**

a) weighty; heavy
b) a formal request
c) the Pope
d) to show through an art form
e) a very small amount of money
f) an advocate
g) a liquid mixture with magical, healing, or poisonous properties
h) someone using a false identity
i) to arrest for a crime; to perceive
j) reverence; devotion to God
k) an instinctive physical desire, especially hunger
l) an act of retaliation
m) preying on others
n) helpless; powerless
o) easily carried or moved
p) capacity to develop for the future
q) especially convenient or appropriate
r) calm; peaceful
s) drinkable
t) to put off until later

Exercise C

ACROSS
1 Characterized by plundering or preying on others
2 The capacity to develop more fully in the future
4 To take into custody; to perceive
6 An advocate; an open supporter
8 Having an undisturbed appearance (of water)
9 An instinctive physical desire, especially for food
11 The pope or a bishop
13 The act of retaliation
15 A formal request to a superior authority for a right or benefit
16 A small amount of money

DOWN
1 Having great weight; labored and dull
3 Suited or right for a particular purpose
5 To represent in a picture or sculpture
7 A person who deceives by taking a false identity
10 Weak; helpless; powerless
11 Easily carried or moved
12 A drink with healing, magical, or poisonous powers
14 Drinkable
15 Reverence or devotion to God

Lesson XIX

PRESS-, PUNG-, PUNI-, PUT-, RAP-, RATIO,
REG-, RID-, ROG-, ROTA, RUPT-

PRESS-	**PUNG-**	**PUNI-**	**PUT-**	**RAP-**	**RATIO**
to press	to puncture	to punish	to think	to seize	account

REC-, REG-	**RID-**	**ROG-**	**ROTA**	**RUPT-**
to rule, govern	to laugh	to ask, beg	wheel	to break

> *oppress, pungent, punish, amputate, compute, rapture, ratio, rational, rationale, rectify, rector, regular, ridicule, deride, arrogant, derogatory, interrogate, interrogative, rotate, interrupt, rupture*

Word Definitions

oppress   **v.** to keep down by unjust authority
"Slaves were oppressed by demanding masters and backbreaking work."

oppression (n.), oppressive (adj.)
oppressus (past participle of *opprimere* to press against)

pungent
adj. biting or caustic to the taste or smell
"'A Modest Proposal' was Swift's pungent satire of English attitudes toward Ireland."
pungere to prick; to puncture

punish
v. to inflict a penalty on as retribution for an offense
"Psychologists claim that to punish by spanking is to invite more aggressive behavior."
punishment (n.)
punire to punish < *poena* penalty

amputate
v. to cut off a part of the body, usually a limb or digit
"The onset of gangrene in his leg required amputation below the knee."
amputation (n.)
amputare to cut around: *am-, ambi-* around + *putare* to cut

compute
v. to determine by mathematics; to determine by arithmetic or mathematical reasoning
"One computes on an abacus by pushing beads along wires stretched in a rigid frame."
computation (n.)
computare to reckon; to calculate: *com-* together + *putare* to think; to believe

rapture
n. a feeling of intense pleasure or joy; the state of being carried away
"At first news of the award, a Nobel prize winner must feel utter rapture."
rapere to seize; to carry off

ratio
n. the quantitative relation between two amounts, showing the number of times one value contains or is contained within the other
"The Golden Ratio of 1.618, symbolized as Φ, underlies the graceful proportions of Greek architecture."
ratio account; reckoning

rational
adj. based on or in accordance with reason or logic
"To an economist, 'rational action' may be either sensible or efficient, or both."
rationality (n.)
rationalis possessing reason (adj.); theoretician (n.) < *ratio* account; reckoning

rationale
n. a set of reasons or a logical basis for a course of action or a belief
"The rationale for the Panama Canal was economy of time and money in shipping."
rationalis possessing reason (adj.); theoretician (n.) < *ratio* account; reckoning

rectify
v. to put right; to correct
"The situation was a lost cause and therefore impossible to rectify."

rectificare to make right: *rectus* right + *ficare* to make; to do (variant of *facere*)

rector	n. a priest or member of the clergy in charge of a church "A rector, or leader of a church or parish, lives in a rectory." *rector* ruler < *regere* to rule
regular	adj. arranged in a consistent or definite pattern; recurring at short intervals; conforming to or governed by an accepted standard of procedure or convention "The Redcoats were regular soldiers, while the Colonials were an irregular militia." *regula* rule
ridicule	n. mockery or derision "Puritans with their feet locked in wooden stocks called pillories were objects of public ridicule." v. subject to mockery "When Jenny walked in the classroom with a polka dotted vest and trousers, she was immediately ridiculed by her friends." *ridiculum* laughable; absurd < *ridere* to laugh at
deride	v. to express contempt for; to ridicule; to speak scornfully or scoff at (someone) "Elizabethan audiences derided unpopular actors with boos and nasty epithets." *deridere* to scoff at: *de-* down, from + *ridere* to laugh at
arrogant	adj. having an exaggerated sense of one's own importance or abilities "The US is viewed by many as an arrogant, vain, and boastful nation." arrogance (n.) *arrogare* to claim for oneself: *ad-* to + *rogare* to ask
derogatory	adj. showing a critical or disrespectful attitude toward; disparaging "Many gourmets make derogatory remarks about the quality of fast food, but some secretly indulge." *derogare* to diminish or detract: *de-* aside, away + *rogare* to ask; to invite
interrogate	v. to ask questions aggressively "The Inquisition was notorious for interrogating prisoners on pain of torture." interrogation (n.) *interrogare* to question: *inter-* between + *rogare* to ask
interrogative	adj. having the force of a question; questioning "The interrogative arch of his eyebrows showed his disbelief." *interrogare* to question: *inter-* between + *rogare* to ask
rotate	v. to move in a circle around an axis; to move regularly in and out of (something) "Before becoming hotel manager, she rotated through several menial jobs to understand the challenges faced by the employees she would supervise." rotation (n.)

rotare to turn in a circle

interrupt v. to stop the continuous progress of; to break the continuity of
"Morse code was sent by interrupted pulses of electricity through telegraph wires."
interruption (n.)
interrumpere to break; to interrupt: *inter* between + *rumpere* to break

rupture v. to break or burst suddenly; to breach or disturb
"Spherical bombs bouncing off the water's surface hit and ruptured the Ruhr dams."
n. an instance of bursting
"A rupture of the Achilles tendon can keep an athlete out for an entire season."
ruptus broken (past participle of *rumpere* to break)

Exercise A

Use the word box at the beginning of the lesson to fill in the blanks below:

1. On the mathematics test, I was not sure whether to express the answer as a percentage or a _____.

2. When he walked out of the prison and was embraced by his wife, he felt complete _____.

3. The demonstrators tried to _____ Wall Street by blocking traffic.

4. A _____ polygon is one whose sides are all of equal length.

5. After centuries of being _____, first as slaves and then through Jim Crow laws and lynchings, black Americans organized boycotts and demonstrations to win full legal equality.

6. Bill O'Reilly acts _____ and self-serving when interviewing guests on his show.

7. The dealer recommended that the new owner should _____ the tires every 5,000 miles.

8. When you bump into something, some capillaries will _____, resulting in a bruise.

9. The professor explained his _____ for requiring three papers in one week.

10. Whether by hand or machine, he was required to _____ the store's receipts and expenses daily.

11. Even though the surgeon was able to spare the patient's life, she was forced to _____ his arm.

12. In English grammar, an _____ sentence should not be confused with either an affirmative or negative one.

13. Little children have a tendency to tease and _____ those who are different.

14. He felt badly that he had gotten his co-worker in trouble, and tried to _____ the situation by taking the blame himself.

15. The hoarder's house was filled with the _____ odor of cat and dog feces.

16. If you could explain the problem in a logical, _____ way, I think I could help you solve it.

17. The police began to _____ the suspect by asking where he was when the crime occurred.

18. To _____ drunken drivers, judges can suspend their licenses or put them in jail for repeat offenses.

19. To feel better about themselves, sometimes people make _____ remarks about others.

20. The _____ greeted the members of the congregation as they exited the church.

21. He was respectful to his boss's face, but liked to _____ him behind his back, calling him an incompetent idiot.

Exercise B

Match the word with the letter of its definition:

1. ____ **amputate**
2. ____ **arrogant**
3. ____ **compute**
4. ____ **derogatory**
5. ____ **interrogate**
6. ____ **interrogative**
7. ____ **interrupt**
8. ____ **oppress**
9. ____ **pungent**
10. ____ **punish**
11. ____ **rapture**
12. ____ **ratio**
13. ____ **rational**
14. ____ **rationale**
15. ____ **rectify**
16. ____ **rector**
17. ____ **regular**
18. ____ **ridicule**
19. ____ **rotate**
20. ____ **rupture**
21. ____ **deride**

a) to put right
b) sensible; logical
c) to inflict a penalty for a wrong
d) the priest in charge of a church
e) to question aggressively
f) a quantitative relationship between two amounts
g) to cut off a limb or digit
h) questioning
i) to determine by mathematics
j) critical and disrespectful
k) to move in a circle around an axis
l) strong and unpleasant to the smell or taste
m) to disturb; to halt something
n) a logical basis for a belief or course of action
o) to keep down unjustly
p) having an exaggerated sense of one's importance
q) to mock
r) intense joy
s) arranged in a consistent pattern; occurring at consistent intervals
t) to speak of someone with scorn
u) to burst suddenly

Exercise C

ACROSS
4 To ask questions aggressively
6 Showing a critical or disrespectful attitude
8 To keep down by unjust authority
12 To cut off a part of the body
14 A priest or member of the clergy in charge of a church
17 To stop continuous progress; to break continuity
19 A feeling of intense pleasure or joy
20 Biting or caustic to the taste or smell

DOWN
1 Having an exaggerated sense of one's own importance or abilities
2 Having the force of a question; a question
3 To express contempt for; to ridicule, to scorn

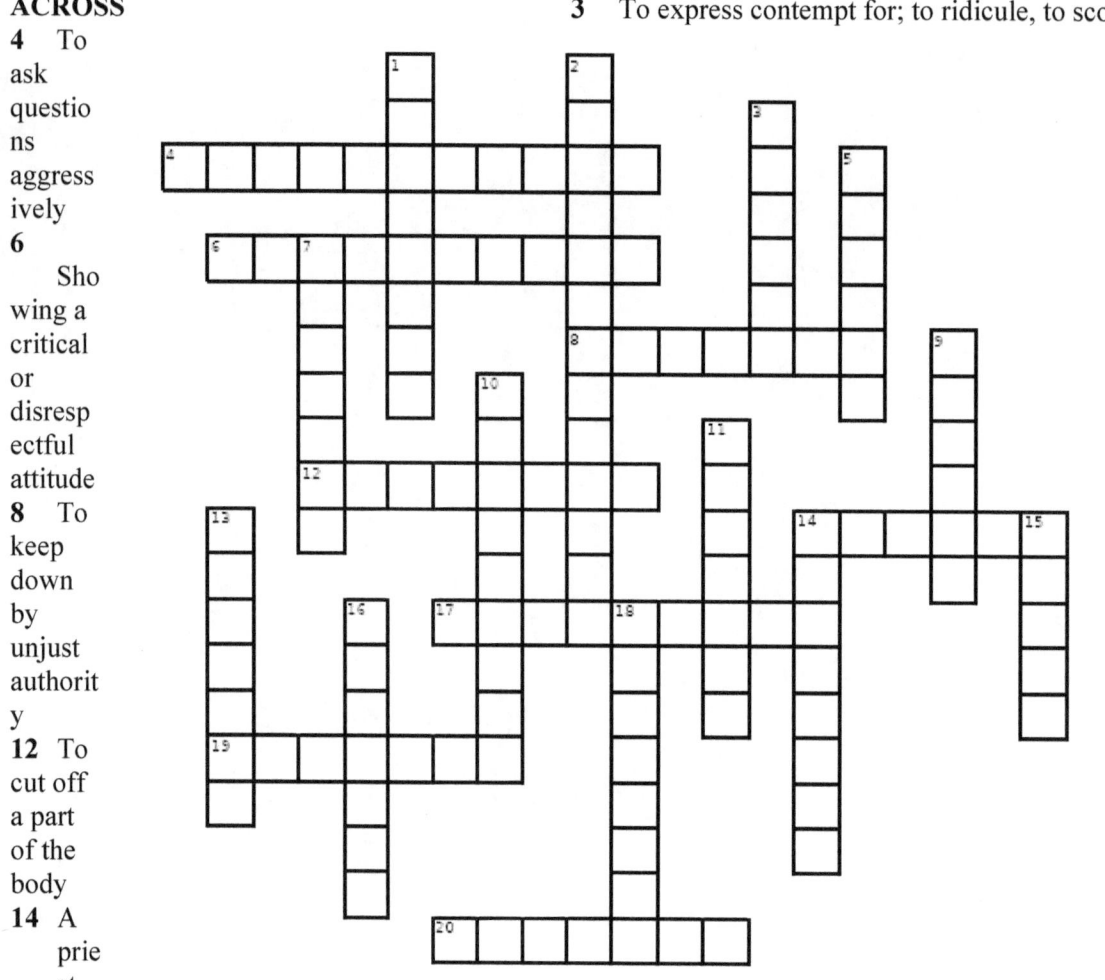

5 To inflict a penalty on as retribution for an offense
7 Arranged in a consistent or definite pattern; recurring at short intervals
9 To move in a circle around an axis
10 A set of reasons or a logical basis for a course of action or a belief
11 To determine by mathematics
13 To break or burst suddenly; to breach or to disturb
14 Based on or in accordance with reason or logic
15 The quantitative relation between two amounts showing the number of times one value contains or is contained within the other
16 To put right; to correct
18 Mockery or derision

Lesson XX

SACR-, SALI-, SALIS, SANGUIS, SATIS,

SCRIB-, SECT-, SEQUI, SED-, SENSIS, SENS-

SACR-	SALI-, SALT-	SALIS	SANGUIS	SATIS	SCRIB-
holy	to jump	salt	blood	enough	to write

SECT-	SEQUI	SED-, SESS-	SENSIS	SENS-, SENT-
to cut	to follow	to sit	old	to think

> *sacrament, sacred, assail, assault, saline, sanguine, satiate,
> prescribe, manuscript, dissect, segment, consecutive, consequence, sequel,
> sequence, session, senile, consensus, resent, sensory*

Word Definitions

sacrament   **n.** a religious ceremony or ritual regarded as imparting divine grace, such as baptism, communion, or marriage
"Seven sacraments or holy rites as instituted by Catholics are described in the New Testament."
sacramentum sacrament: *sacra* holy; religious rite + *mentum* mind; intention

sacred   **adj.** connected with a deity and so deserving veneration; holy
"The Holy Grail is the legendary sacred cup used by Christ and his disciples at the Last Supper."
sacra, sacrata holy

assail   **v.** to make a concerted or violent attack on; to attack verbally
"Armor-piercing English longbow arrows assailed the French knights at Agincourt."
salire to leap

assault   **n.** a violent attack or threat of harm; an aggressive attempt to do something demanding
"The bank robber could not be charged with assault since the teller did not feel threatened."
v. to make an attack on; to threaten
"The missiles assaulted the aircraft carrier."
saltus a jump; a sudden move < *salire* to leap

saline   **adj.** containing or impregnated with salt
"Seawater and blood are both saline fluids."
sal salt

sanguine   **adj.** cheerfully optimistic or hopeful; blood-red; bloody
"An optimist by nature, the recent graduate was sanguine about his job prospects,
despite the recession."

sanguis blood

satiate
v. to satisfy fully
"The tea and hors d'oeuvres served at the garden party failed to satiate his hunger."
satiare to satisfy; to nourish < *satis* enough

prescribe
v. to advise and to authorize the use of, especially in writing; to state authoritatively that something should be done in a particular way
"The conductor prescribed which pieces the orchestra would perform that night."
prescription (n.)
praescribere to direct in writing: *prae-* before + *scribere* to write

manuscript
a handwritten document or piece of music; the original of a document
"Once, novelists sent a penned manuscript to their publishers; now they e-mail Word documents."
manus hand + *scriptus* written (past participle of scribere to write)

dissect
v. to methodically cut up in order to study its internal parts; to analyze in minute detail
"*The Decline and Fall of the Roman Empire* dissects the causes of Rome's demise."
dissection (n.)
dissecare to cut apart: *de-* away from + *secare* to cut

segment
n. each of the parts into which something is or may be divided
"The presentation was divided into segments concerning the three major topics."
v. to divide into parts
"Sunday newspapers often carry inserts segmented to geographical areas."
segmentum a cutting; a shred < *secare* to cut

consecutive
adj. following continuously or in order
"Happily, the stock market rose for several consecutive weeks."
consequi to follow closely: *con-* with + *sequi* to follow

consequence
n. a result or effect
"As a consequence of his hard work and loyalty, Dirk Nowitzki won the NBA finals Most Valuable Player award in 2011."
consequi to follow closely: *con-* with + *sequi* to follow

sequel
n. a published broadcast or recorded work that continues the story or develops the theme of an earlier one; an event that follows another
"A thunderclap is a frequent sequel to a lightning bolt."
sequi to follow

sequence
n. a particular order in which related events, movements, etc. follow each other; a series of related events or movements in a particular order
"The sequence of episodes in Joyce's *Ulysses* mirrors Homer's *Odyssey*."

sequential (adj.)
sequi to follow

session n. a period devoted to a particular activity; a meeting of a deliberative or judicial body to conduct its business; the part of a year or a day during which teaching takes place in a school
"Cabinet meetings are conducted in sessions closed to the media."
sessus seated (past participle of *sedere* to sit)

senile adj. having the weakness or diseases of old age; mentally incapacitated by reason of agedness
"One sign that she was becoming senile was that she sometimes sent birthday cards to her grandchildren at Christmas, and vice versa."
senex old man

consensus n. general agreement of a group, with no major dissent
"The subcommittee reached a positive consensus and forwarded the nomination."
consentire to agree: *con-* together + *sentire* to feel

resent v. to feel bitterness or indignation at
"Those who resented Alexander's power may have tried to poison him."
resentment (n.)
re- back + *sentire* to feel

sensory adj. relating to sensation or the senses
"Bank vaults have sensory devices to detect heat, motion, pressure, and sound."
sensorius sensory < *sentire* to feel

Exercise A

Use the word box at the beginning of the lesson to fill in the blanks below:

1. Typically, a high school biology class involves having to _____ a frog.

2. The detective arrested her abusive husband for _____ and battery.

3. When writing a descriptive essay on your environment, make full use of your _____ perception for better prose.

4. During emergencies, paramedics may maintain blood pressure by pumping _____ solution into the patient's blood supply line.

5. In India, the cow is a _____ animal and may not be killed or eaten.

6. Doctors _____ medications that they think will benefit their patients.

7. After much discussion, the tribe reached a _____ on how to punish him: banishment.

8. The President of the United States may serve only two _____ four-year terms in office.

9. An elderly man warned of an alien invasion in Utah, but his words of caution were dismissed as _____ ramblings.

10. The prosecutor laid out the _____ of events minute by minute.

11. Literary scholars love to study the original _____ of their favorite poems, books, and essays, complete with crossings out and marginal notes.

12. Christians may receive the _____ of baptism, usually when they are quite young.

13. After the training _____, they adjourned to a restaurant for dinner.

14. Some Americans _____ having to pay income taxes to the federal government.

15. After their honeymoon, the couple was _____ about their future together.

16. In "Parent Effectiveness Training," children should be given natural or logical _____ for their mistakes and mischief, such as cleaning up when they spill milk.

17. The success of the movie *Rocky* was never equaled by any of its _____.

18. Many people don't realize that bananas, like oranges, can be split into roughly equal _____.

19. Mitt Romney _____ his chief rival for the Republican presidential nomination, Rick Perry, in speeches and a series of television ads.

20. In European folklore, vampires attack humans with their preternaturally long incisors in order to _____ their thirst for blood.

Exercise B

Match the word with the letter of its definition:

1. ____ assail   a) cheerfully optimistic
2. ____ assault   b) a handwritten book, document, or piece of music
3. ____ consensus   c) a follow-up in a series
4. ____ consecutive   d) to write a prescription; to advise
5. ____ consequence   e) a physical attack or threat of harm
6. ____ dissect   f) to divide into separate parts; a piece
7. ____ manuscript   g) salty in nature
8. ____ prescribe   h) to analyze in minute detail
9. ____ resent   i) a religious ceremony invoking divine grace
10. ____ sacrament   j) to attack
11. ____ sacred   k) relating to sensation or the physical senses
12. ____ saline   l) a general agreement
13. ____ sanguine   m) religious; holy
14. ____ satiate   n) to hold a grudge
15. ____ segment   o) a meeting
16. ____ senile   p) a particular order
17. ____ sensory   q) successive; following immediately after
18. ____ sequel   r) to satisfy to the full
19. ____ sequence   s) mentally feeble due to old age
20. ____ session   t) the result of an action

Exercise C

ACROSS

1. A result or effect
3. A religious ceremony or ritual regarded as imparting divine grace
5. A particular order in which related events follow each other
6. Connected with a deity and so deserving veneration; holy
7. To methodically cut up in order to study its internal parts
10. To advise and to authorize the use of, especially in writing
12. To make a concerted or violent attack on
13. A period devoted to a particular activity
15. Each of the parts into which something is or may be divided
16. To feel bitterness or indignation against someone
17. A published work that continues the story of an earlier one

DOWN

1. General agreement
2. Following continuously
4. A violent attack or threat of harm
6. Cheerfully optimistic; hopeful
8. Fully satisfy
9. Containing or impregnated with salt
11. Relating to sensation or the senses
14. Having the weakness or diseases of old age

Quiz 4

> mountain, opportune, interrupt, punish, proponent,
> sacraments, amputate, impeccable, derogatory, placid,
> muster, sacred, annihilate, oppress, sanguine, ridicule,
> consensus, resent, potential, consequence, consecutive

1. I _____ all my energy and strength to climb the steep _____.

2. The first atomic bomb used in World War II _____ Hiroshima; the second decimated Nagasaki.

3. A _____ of nonviolent action, Gandhi led massive protest actions that helped India win independence from Great Britain.

4. The diplomat's joke did not come at an _____ time; the peace conference participants were too angry to laugh.

5. "Your summits are clear; the sky and lake are blue and _____." – *Frankenstein*, by Mary Shelley.

6. The young law school graduate demonstrated great _____, and she also had an _____ academic record.

7. After a shark mauled his foot and calf beyond repair, the doctors decided to _____ his leg below the knee.

8. Sheriffs and judges throughout the South colluded to _____ African-Americans and _____ them if they stepped out of line.

9. The student was _____ when she arrived at the formal dance in a home-sewn dress.

10. The comment was not only offensive and _____; it _____ the speaker's presentation, causing her to lose her train of thought.

11. The Seven _____ are _____ to Catholics around the world.

12. Despite two _____ years of losses, the CEO had a _____ feeling that the company's performance would turn around.

13. The _____ among the top executives was to expand by adding more stores.

14. He was spanked for the least misbehavior, a _____ so severe that he _____ his mother all his life.

Lesson XXI

SIMIL-, SOLUS, SOLV-, SOMN-, SON, SPARG-, SPEC-

SIMIL-, SIMUL-
similar, same

SOLUS
alone

SOLV-, SOLUT-
to loosen

SOMN-
to sleep

SON
sound

SPARG-
to scatter

SPEC-, SPECT-, SPIC-
to look at

> *simile, simulate, simultaneous, solitude, solo, absolute, dissolve, resolve, resolution, insomnia, resonate, sonar, supersonic, aspersion, disperse, despicable, perspective, spectacle, spectator, spectrum*

Word Definitions

simile
n. a figure of speech involving the comparison of one thing with another thing of a different kind.
"'Her smile dawned like a summer's morn' is a simile."
similis like; similar

simulate
v. to imitate or to reproduce the appearance, character, or conditions of
"Heartburn can simulate a heart attack, so a medical consultation is warranted."
simulation (n.)
simulare to copy; to represent

simultaneous
adj. occurring, operating, or done at the same time
"Thomas Jefferson and John Adams died almost simultaneously on July 4, 1826."
simul at the same time; at once

solitude
n. the state of being alone
"A hermit or recluse prefers a life of solitude."
solus alone

solo
n. a piece of music, song, or dance for a single performer; an unaccompanied flight by a pilot
"'O sole mio!' is a well-known operatic solo popularized by Enrico Caruso."
adj./adv. for or done by one person
"It was a magnificent solo performance."
v. to perform solo
"He soloed only after passing the written exam for a pilot's license."
solus alone

130

absolute   **adj.** complete or total; complete in nature, not relative or comparative
"At a temperature of absolute zero, molecules cease movement."
n. a value or principle regarded as universally valid or able to be viewed without relation to other things
"One philosophy insists on absolutes; its counterpart holds that all things are relative."
absolutus (past participle of *absolvere* to set free; to pay off: *ab-* from + *solvere* to loosen)

dissolve   **v.** to become or to cause to become incorporated into a liquid so as to form a solution; to formally end an assembly or annul a marriage
"Annulment is the Catholic alternative to divorce as a means to dissolve a marriage."
n. an instance of dissolving from one image or scene in a film to another
"The fight scene slowly dissolved into a scene of the family at home together."
dissolvere to dissolve; to melt: *dis-* apart + *solvere* to loosen or solve

resolve   **v.** to settle or find a solution to; to decide firmly on a course of action; to gain clarity (as in a photographic negative)
"A detective's task is to follow clues and evidence to resolve a crime."
n. a firm determination
"Michael Jordan had the resolve to win the game, despite having the flu."
resolvere to release; to relax: *re-* (intensive force) + *solvere* to loosen

resolution   **n.** the formal quality of being decided or determined; a firm decision; the settling of a problem or dispute
"Many New Year's resolutions to change habits or behavior are quickly broken."
resolute (adj.)
resolvere to release; to relax: *re-* (intensive force) + *solvere* to loosen

insomnia   **n.** habitual sleeplessness
"Insomnia is rarely a problem for cats, who sleep about 18 hours daily."
insomnis sleepless < *somnus, somni* sleep

resonate   **adj.** continuing to sound, ring, or reverberate; having the ability to evoke enduring images, memories or emotions
"A yodel resonates in the Alps."
resonare to resound: *re-* again + *sonare* to sound

sonar   **n.** a system for the detection of objects under water, based on the emission and measured reflection of sound pulses; the method of echolocation used in air or water by animals such as bats and whales
"A car equipped with sonar automatically stays a safe distance behind a forward car."
so(und) na(vigation and) r(anging) < *sonare* to sound; to make noise

supersonic   **adj.** involving or denoting a speed greater than the speed of sound
"Traveling faster than sound, the Concorde was an SST, or supersonic transport."
super above; in addition + *sonitus* noise; sound

aspersion	**n.** a withering attack on someone's or something's character or reputation "The prosecuting attorney cast aspersions on the witness's character and credibility." *aspergere* to sprinkle; to splatter; to stain
disperse	**v.** to scatter in different directions or over a wide area "At Lexington, a Redcoat officer cried out to the militiamen: 'Disperse, ye rebels!'" *dispergere* to scatter about
despicable	**adj.** deserving hatred and contempt "In wartime, a traitor is perhaps the most despicable of men." *despicari* to despise; to scorn: *de-* down + *specere* to look at
perspective	**n.** (1) the art of portraying three-dimensional objects on a two-dimensional surface to indicate their height, width, depth, and position in relation to each other when viewed from a particular point of view "Renaissance painters used perspective to create more realistic art." **n.** (2) point of view "The story would look quite different from the villain's perspective." *perspicere* to look through; to examine: *per-* through + *specere* to look at
spectacle	**n.** a visually striking performance or display "Nero's Coliseum was an arena for spectacles including gladiatorial contests and wild animals." *specere* to look at
spectator	**n.** a person who watches at a show, game, or other event "At some soccer fields, players are protected from the spectators by a moat." *specere* to look at
spectrum	**n.** a band of colors produced by a separation of the components of light by their different degrees of refraction according to wavelength (as in a rainbow); a scale extending between two points; a range "The spectrum of European political opinion ranges from communist to neo-Nazi." *specere* to look at

Exercise A

Use the word box at the beginning of the lesson to fill in the blanks below:

1. The Cubists upended the rules of _____ in painting by portraying the same object from several points of view simultaneously.

2. "Power tends to corrupt; _____ power corrupts absolutely": so said Lord Acton, a British historian.

3. If you cast unjustified _____ on my character, I will sue you for libel.

4. I hope the sun will _____ the fog.

5. Teenage students sometimes benefit from _____ right-brain and left-brain stimulation, such as listening to music while doing their homework.

6. The United Nations _____ had no legal force, but expressed the world's overwhelming condemnation of the ongoing genocide.

7. NASA space camp has computers that _____ space flight, so campers can experience the challenges and sensations of space travel without leaving Earth.

8. His crimes were so heinous and _____ that even the other prisoners looked down on him.

9. Baking soda _____ in water is an easy home remedy for mild acid indigestion.

10. He fell asleep during the day, but lay awake most of the night, so the doctor prescribed _____ medication.

11. You can be in the midst of a crowd of people and experience loneliness, but not _____.

12. The largest bells of the carillon may _____ for a full minute after they are played.

13. A _____ is a very useful device in poetry and descriptive prose.

14. Military planes were the first to use _____ technology, but some passenger aircraft now do so as well.

15. The circus came to town and provided one tremendous _____ after another, from death-defying acrobats to prancing elephants.

16. A card game that is played _____ is called solitaire.

17. You cannot _____ this dispute matter overnight.

18. Every _____ was entertained by the Sondheim musical, which included television comedian Stephen Colbert in the cast.

19. _____ is used by humans to detect objects under water and by whales to locate each other.

20. A broad _____ of colors made the paint color decision even harder.

Exercise B

Match the word with the letter of its definition:

1. ____ absolute
2. ____ aspersion
3. ____ despicable
4. ____ dissolve
5. ____ disperse
6. ____ insomnia
7. ____ perspective
8. ____ resolution
9. ____ resolve
10. ____ resonate
11. ____ simile
12. ____ simulate
13. ____ simultaneous
14. ____ solitude
15. ____ solo
16. ____ sonar
17. ____ spectacle
18. ____ spectator
19. ____ spectrum
20. ____ supersonic

a) at the same time
b) contemptible
c) to settle; to decide
d) a figure of speech comparing one thing to another
e) faster than the speed of sound
f) complete and total
g) point of view
h) an echolocation system
i) to distribute or spread over a wide area
j) to disappear, deteriorate, or degenerate; to disperse in a liquid
k) an attack on one's reputation
l) an audience member; a bystander
m) inability to sleep
n) the state of being alone
o) to imitate an appearance or action
p) a firm decision
q) to reverberate with sound
r) done by one person alone
s) a fantastic visual display or exhibition
t) a range

Exercise C

ACROSS
1. A visually striking performance or display
3. Habitual sleeplessness
4. Deserving hatred and contempt
6. A system for the detection of objects under-water based on the emission and measured reflection of sound pulses
7. The state of being alone
8. A firm decision; a state of resolve
9. An attack on someone's or something's character or reputation
11. To become incorporated into a liquid so as to form a solution
12. To imitate or to reproduce the appearance of
13. To settle or find a solution to
14. Continuing to sound or ring

DOWN
1. Occurring, operating, or done at the same time
2. A figure of speech involving the comparison of one thing with another
4. To spread in different directions or over a wide area
5. Denoting a speed greater than the speed of sound
6. A person who watches at a show, game, or other event
9. Total and complete
10. A band of colors separated by wavelength, such as the rainbow
12. A piece of music, song, or dance for one performer

Lesson XXII

SPIR-, STAT-, STELLA, STRICT-, STRUCT-, SUAVIS,
SUM-, TANG-, TEMPER-, TEMPOR-

SPIR-	**STAT-**	**STELLA**	**STRICT-**	**STRUCT-**
to breathe	to stand	star	to bind	to build

SUAVIS	**SUM-**	**TANG-**	**TEMPER-**	**TEMPOR-**
delightful	to take; to start	to touch	to combine	time

> *aspire, conspiracy, respiratory, spiritual, constant, constellation, stellar, constrict, construct, instruct, obstruct, suave, presume, tangent, tangible, temper, temperament, contemporary, temporal*

Word Definitions

aspire
v. to direct one's hopes or ambitions toward achieving something
"In 2008 Hillary Clinton aspired to be the first female American president."
aspiration (n.)
aspirare to aspire; to influence: *ad-* to + *spirare* to breathe < *spiritus* breath; soul; life

conspiracy
n. a secret plan by a group to do something harmful or unlawful
"Conspiracy theorists contend that Lee Harvey Oswald did not act alone in the assassination of President Kennedy."
conspire (v.)
conspirare to agree; to plot: *con-* together with + *spirare* to breathe < *spiritus* breath; soul; life

respiratory
adj. relating to or affecting breathing
"Leaves are the main respiratory organ of plants, taking in carbon dioxide and returning oxygen to the atmosphere."
respirare to breathe out; to take breath: *re-* again + *spirare* to breathe

spiritual
adj. relating to or affecting the human spirit, as opposed to material or physical things; relating to religion or religious beliefs
"A priest must tend to the spiritual needs of his parishioners."
spirare to breathe < *spiritus* breath; soul; life

constant
adj. occurring continuously; faithful
"A lover is said to be 'constant' if he or she remains faithful to the beloved."
n. an unchanging situation
"The pain in his lower back was a constant, so he learned to ignore it."
constare to stand firm: *con-* with + *stare* to stand

constellation n. a group of stars forming a recognized pattern and typically named after a mythological or other figure; a similar cluster of related people or objects
"Psychologists treat dysfunctions of the individual within the family constellation."
con- together with + *stella* star

stellar adj. featuring or having the qualities of a star performer; relating to a star or stars
"Nadia Comaneci's performance on the balance beam was stellar, earning her a perfect 10 from the Olympic judges."
stella star

constrict v. to make or become narrower, especially by encircling pressure
"The girdle is no longer in vogue as a means to constrict the waistline."
constrictus tightly bound (past participle of *constringere* to bind together tightly: *con-* together + *stringere* to tie up; to bind)

construct v. to build or erect; to form from various conceptual elements; to form according to grammatical rules
"The builders began to construct the main span of the bridge."
n. an idea or theory; a group of words forming a phrase
"A passive verb construct is used in this very sentence."
construction (n.)
constructus built (past participle of *construere* to heap together; to build: *con-* together + *struere* to pile; to build

instruct v. to direct or command; to teach; to give information to
"The commander instructed his aide to fetch maps of the terrain."
instruction (n.)
instruere to build upon; to teach: *in-* upon, towards + *struere* to pile up; to build

obstruct v. to be in the way of; to prevent or hinder
"After a hurricane, downed trees frequently obstruct the roadways."
obstruction (n.)
obstructus blocked up (past participle of *obstruere* to block up: *ob-* against + *struere* to pile up; to build)

suave adj. charming, confident, and elegant
"James Bond is portrayed as a suave, sophisticated man with lightning reflexes."
suavis agreeable; attractive

presume v. to suppose that something is the case on the basis of probability
"Dr. Livingstone, I presume?' were *New York Herald* reporter D. M. Stanley's words upon meeting the famed explorer in a village on Lake Tanganyika."
presumption (n.)
praesumere to anticipate: *prae-* before + *sumere* to take; to suppose

tangent	**n.** a straight line or plane that touches a curve or curved surface at a single point or along a line; an irrelevant topic of conversation "To 'go off on a tangent' is to digress wildly from the topic at hand." **adj.** touching but not intersecting "That line is tangent to the circle." *tangere* to touch
tangible	**adj.** discernible by touch; palpable; possible to be treated as fact; possible to understand or realize "Material evidence refers to tangible clues." *tangere* to touch
temper	**n.** a person's state of mind or emotions; disposition; a tendency to become easily angry or irritable; an outbreak of anger "The foreman was known for his temper, so his team worked hard and kept their heads down." **v.** to moderate; to bring to a desired consistency, texture or hardness; to harden or strengthen by application of heat or by heating and cooling; to strengthen through experience or hardship; to toughen "His enthusiasm for shark fishing was tempered by an appreciation of its dangers." *temperare* to mingle; to restrain
temperament	**n.** the manner of thinking, behaving, or reacting typical of a specific person; excessive irritability or sensitivity "He had an easy temperament, but his brother was an impatient man." *temperare* to mingle; to restrain
contemporary	**adj.** (1) belonging to the same period of time; about the same age The *Mona Lisa* is contemporary to the paintings on the ceiling of the Sistine Chapel." **adj.** (2) current; modern "The Metropolitan Museum features both historical and contemporary art." **n.** a person of similar age "Abraham Lincoln was a contemporary of Charles Darwin; in fact, they were born on the same day." *con-* together with + *tempus, temporis* time; weather; season
temporal	**adj.** (1) limited by time; worldly; lasting only for a time; not eternal; secular or lay "Christians believe one's temporal life is followed by an eternal one." *tempus, temporis* time; weather; season

Exercise A

Use the word box at the beginning of the lesson to fill in the blanks below:

1. Ideals are abstract, but actions are a _____ measure of someone's true values.

2. They were quite disappointed when they realized the new house across the street would _____ their ocean view.

3. The real estate agent was searching for a large _____ house, as his clients had an extensive modern art collection they wanted to display in suitable surroundings.

4. Many young boys _____ to become professional athletes, but few realize their dreams.

5. Girlfriends may come and go, but my dog, Tara, is my _____ companion.

6. I did not wish to _____ the outcome, so I waited patiently until the movie ended.

7. The cat tried to claw off her collar, which was so tight that it _____ her breathing.

8. The mosque is my _____ home.

9. Golden and Labrador retrievers are especially known for their calm _____.

10. Audra McDonald gave a _____ performance as Bess in Gershwin's beloved musical, "Porgy and Bess."

11. A _____ disease would cause breathing difficulties.

12. To the disappointment of the spectators and the rest of the team, the pitcher walked off the mound in fit of _____.

13. The architect drew up a basic colonial house design the builder could _____ in less than six months and easily adapt to different families' needs.

14. _____ affairs relate to the secular side of things, as opposed to the religious side.

15. There was a _____ to manipulate the results of the election.

16. She went off on a _____, but it was so fascinating that no one tried to steer the discussion back to the original topic.

17. Your costume should show what a _____ man your character is.

18. There are 88 named _____, according to modern astronomers.

19. They were waiting for the teacher to _____ them on proper CPR procedure.

139

Exercise B

Match the word with the letter of its definition:

1. ____ **aspire**
2. ____ **conspiracy**
3. ____ **constant**
4. ____ **constellation**
5. ____ **constrict**
6. ____ **construct**
7. ____ **contemporary**
8. ____ **instruct**
9. ____ **obstruct**
10. ____ **presume**
11. ____ **respiratory**
12. ____ **spiritual**
13. ____ **stellar**
14. ____ **suave**
15. ____ **tangent**
16. ____ **tangible**
17. ____ **temper**
18. ____ **temperament**
19. ____ **temporal**

a) involving the stars
b) to suppose
c) nonmaterial; religious
d) touchable
e) to build; to erect
f) a group of stars
g) to hope to accomplish
h) a line that touches a curve at one point
i) secular; material
j) to block
k) a secret plot involving more than one person
l) to teach
m) unchanging
n) disposition
o) to make narrower
p) modern
q) affecting breathing or respiration
r) charming and elegant
s) a fit of rage

Exercise C

ACROSS
1. Lasting for only a time; not eternal
4. The manner of thinking, behaving, or reacting typical of a specific person
6. Featuring or having the qualities of a star performer
7. Relating to or affecting the human spirit, as opposed to material or physical things
8. Charming, confident, and elegant
10. To make or become narrower, especially by tightening
13. A group of stars forming a recognized pattern
15. Discernible by the touch; palpable
17. Occurring continuously
18. To direct one's hopes or ambitions toward achieving something
19. To build or erect

DOWN
2. To block, prevent, or hinder
3. Relating to or affecting breathing
5. To moderate
9. A secret plan by a group to do something harmful or unlawful
11. Current; living or occurring at the same time
12. To suppose that something is the case on the basis of probability
14. Touching but not intersecting
16. To direct or command; to teach; to give information to

Lesson XXIII

TEN-, TERM-, TERR-, TEX-, TORS-, TOTUS,
TRACT-, TRUD-, TURB-, ULTIMA, UPT-, UND-

TEN-, TIN-	*TERM-*	*TERR-*	*TEX-*	*TORS-, TORT-*	*TOTUS*
to hold	end	land, earth	to weave	to twist	total

TRACT-	*TRUD-, TRUS-*	*TURB-*	*ULTIMA*	*UPT-*	*UND-*
to drag, pull	to push, shove	to disturb	the last	to break	to wave

> *pertain, pertinent, terminate, extraterrestrial, Mediterranean, subterranean, terrain, context, contort, distort, totalitarian, detract, extract, intrude, turbid, ultimate, ultimatum, corrupt, abundant, redundant*

Word Definitions

pertain v. to have reference to; to relate; to belong as an adjunct part, holding or quality; to be fitting or suitable
"Rules and laws do not pertain to a dictator who is above the law."
pertinere to pertain; to extend to: *per-* thoroughly + *tenere* to hold

pertinent adj. having precise logical relevance to the matter at hand
"A court permits only arguments and evidence pertinent to the guilt or innocence of the accused."
pertinere to pertain; to extend to: *per-* thoroughly + *tenere* to hold

terminate v. to bring to an end or to halt; to occur at or form the end of; to conclude or finish; to discontinue the employment of
"The insubordinate employee was promptly terminated."
termination (n.)
terminus end

extraterrestrial adj. originating, located, or occurring outside Earth or its atmosphere
"Meteors are extraterrestrial objects that usually burn up in Earth's atmosphere."
n. an extraterrestrial life form
"In Steven Spielberg's classic movie, E.T. was an extraterrestrial who accidentally landed on Earth."
extra- beyond + *terra* earth

mediterranean adj. surrounded nearly or completely by dry land
"The Caspian Sea is in fact a mediterranean lake."
n. (capital M) of or relating to the Mediterranean Sea and the countries along it
"Greece's is surrounded on three sides by the Mediterranean Sea."
mediterraneus inland: *medius* middle + *terra* earth

subterranean	**adj.** situated or operating beneath the earth's surface; underground; hidden; secret "The gold sarcophagus of Tutankhamen was discovered in a subterranean tomb." *subterraneus* subterranean: *sub-* sub- + *terra* land
terrain	**n.** an area of land; ground; a particular geographic area; a region; the surface features of an area of land; topography "Topographical maps show the various elevations in a given terrain." *terrenus* of the earth < *terra* earth
context	**n.** the part of a text or statement that surrounds a particular word or passage and determines its meaning; a setting "Sometimes you can determine the meaning of an unfamiliar word from its context." *contextual (adj.), contextualize (v.)* *contexere* to join together: *com-, con-* together + *texere* to weave
contort	**v.** to twist, wrench, or bend severely out of shape; to become twisted into a strained shape or expression "The pretzel is a contorted piece of dough that is salted and baked." *contortion (n.)* *contortus* twisted around (past participle of *contorquere,* to twist round: *com-, con-* together + *torquere* to twist)
distort	**v.** to twist out of a proper or natural relation of parts; to misshape; to misrepresent; to pervert "The claim that slavery alone led to the Civil War distorts a more complex truth." *distortus* misshapen (past participle of *distorquere*: *dis-* away from + *torquere* to twist)
totalitarian	**adj.** a form of government in which the political authority exercises absolute and centralized control over all aspects of life "Communist China is governed by a totalitarian regime, although some aspects of central control have eased in recent years." *totus, tota* total; all; whole
detract	**v.** to draw or take away from; to reduce the value, importance, or quality of something "The offshore wind farm detracted from the view of an unobstructed seascape." *detractus* removed; omitted (past participle of *detrahere* to remove: *de-* away + *trahere* to pull; to draw)

extract v. to draw or pull out; to obtain despite resistance; to remove from separate consideration or publication; to excerpt; to derive or obtain from a source; to derive from an experience
"The neurosurgeon carefully extracted a bullet from the patient's brain."
n. an excerpt or concentrated essence of a substance
"Peppermint extract is used to flavor gum, ice cream, and candy."
extraction (n.)
extractus extracted; removed (past participle of *extrahere* to draw out: *ex-* out + *trahere* to draw; to pull)

intrude v. to put or force in inappropriately, especially without invitation or permission; to enter as an improper or unwanted element
"The sound of her son's rock band practicing intruded on the reader's concentration."
intrusion (n.)
intrudere to thrust in: *in-* into + *trudere* to thrust

turbid adj. having sediment or foreign particles stirred up or suspended; muddy; in a state of turmoil; muddled
"The motorboat left a turbid wake in the shallow pond."
turbidus disordered < *turba* a crowd; a disturbance

ultimate adj. being or happening at the end of a process; being the best or most extreme example of its kind
"The Medal of Honor is the ultimate decoration awarded in the American military."
ultimare to come to an end

ultimatum n. a final offer or statement of terms made by one party to another
"Attila's ultimatum to the Roman town defenders was to surrender or be slaughtered."
ultimare to come to an end

corrupt adj. marked by immorality and perversion; depraved; dishonest; containing errors or alterations
"Not long ago, elections in West Virginia were highly corrupt: In many towns, a man's vote could be bought for a bottle of liquor."
v. to debase; to bribe someone or otherwise compromise their ethics
"Juvenile offenders should never be housed with adult criminals, who will only corrupt them further."
corruption (n.)
corruptus bribed; destroyed (past participle of *corrumpere*: *cor-* altogether + *rumpere* to break)

abundant adj. plentiful; rich
"A bumper crop is an abundant harvest."
abundance (n.)
abundare to abound; to exceed: *ab-* away + *undare* to flow; to surge

redundant	**adj.** exceeding what is necessary or natural; needlessly repetitive or verbose; superfluous
	"The radio talk show caller's comments were redundant; every point he made had already been discussed by someone else."
	redundancy (n.)
	redundare to overflow; to be too numerous: *re-, red-* again + *undare* to flow

Exercise A

Use the word box at the beginning of the lesson to fill in the blanks below:

1. The _____ Diet is very healthy because it emphasizes fresh fruits and vegetables, fish and olive oil.

2. The kidnappers gave the man's employer an _____: pay the $1 million ransom or he would die.

3. Taking a calcium supplement within 48 hours of a bone density test can _____ the results.

4. An alarming number of Americans believe they have been abducted by UFOs and studied by _____.

5. The professor appreciated that the students asked only questions _____ to the topic at hand.

6. Politicians who are caught saying something embarrassing frequently blame the newspaper reporters cover them, saying, "I was quoted out of _____!"

7. Their _____ aim was to force the resignation of the unpopular university president.

8. A _____ regime seeks to dominate its citizens through a combination of terror and thought control.

9. Spelunking in _____ caves is an interesting but sometimes dangerous hobby.

10. We have an _____ supply of fish, lobsters, and shrimp, thanks to strict fishing regulations.

11. All _____ vehicles, or ATV's, are gaining in popularity, even as hiking and camping decline.

12. The entertainment media _____ on the private lives of rock stars and celebrities to a disturbing degree.

13. The contractor threatened to _____ the project if they did not pay their first bill immediately.

14. His crass remarks _____ from an otherwise genteel dinner party.

15. William Shockley's racist theories about genetics were widely disparaged because they did not _____ to the research that won him the Nobel Prize in Physics.

16. He did not want his 16-year-old daughter to date the 19-year-old high school dropout, because he feared the young man would _____ her.

17. In the United Kingdom, they refer to a person who is laid off as being "_____," because their skills or tasks are no longer needed.

18. The accomplished yoga teacher could _____ her limbs into extraordinary poses, leading her students to nickname her "The Human Pretzel."

19. The dentist would only _____ a tooth as a last resort.

20. The _____ waters of Pomp's Pond are not translucent.

Exercise B

Match the word with the letter of its definition:

1. ____ abundant
2. ____ context
3. ____ contort
4. ____ corrupt
5. ____ detract
6. ____ distort
7. ____ extract
8. ____ extraterrestrial
9. ____ intrude
10. ____ Mediterranean
11. ____ pertain
12. ____ pertinent
13. ____ redundant
14. ____ subterranean
15. ____ terminate
16. ____ terrain
17. ____ totalitarian
18. ____ turbid
19. ____ ultimate
20. ____ ultimatum

a) characteristic of the Mediterranean Sea
b) to pull out; to remove
c) a final statement of terms
d) relevant
e) to twist
f) plentiful
g) to bring to an end
h) a stretch of land; surface characteristics of the land
i) to belittle
j) frame of reference
k) to enter without permission
l) autocratic
m) dishonest; unethical
n) to pull out of shape
o) alien; originating outside the earth and its atmosphere
p) to relate to
q) unnecessary; repetitive
r) eventual; final
s) murky
t) below the earth's surface

Exercise C

ACROSS

4 To pull out of a proper or natural relation of parts; to misshape
7 To bring to an end
11 Surrounded nearly or completely by dry land
14 Situated or operating beneath the earth's surface
15 Having sediment or foreign particles stirred up and suspended
19 A form of government in which the political authority exercises absolute and centralized control over all aspects of life
20 To draw or take away from

DOWN

1 The part of a text or statement that a surrounds a particular word
2 Originating, located, or occurring outside Earth
3 To twist or bend
5 Plentiful
6 An area of land; ground; a particular geographic area
8 Exceeding what is necessary or natural
9 Marked by immorality and perversion; depraved; dishonest or unethical
10 Having precise logical relevance to the matter at hand
12 To have reference to; to relate to; to belong as an adjunct part
13 To put or force in inappropriately, especially without invitation
16 A final statement of terms made by one party to another
17 To draw or pull out; to obtain despite resistance
18 Being the best or most extreme example of its kind

Lesson XXIV

URBS, VAC-, VAD-, VAL-, VENDIC-,
VENI-, VENTUS, VER-, VERBUM, VERS-

URBS city	**VAC-** to empty	**VAD-, VAS-** to go	**VAL-** to be strong	**VENDIC-** to avenge
VENI- to come	**VENTUS** wind	**VER-, VERA-, VERI-** truth	**VERBUM** word	**VERS-, VERT-** to turn

> *urban, urbane, evacuate, vacant, evasive, invasion, prevail, vindicate,
> vindictive, advent, event, vent, verify, verity, verbal, verbose,
> adversity, controversy, diversion*

Word Definitions

urban
    adj. of or located in a city; characteristic of the city or city life
    "Urban dwellers forgo the fresh air and broad lawns of the outlying suburbs in exchange for convenience and culture."
    urbs, urbis city

urbane
    adj. polite, refined, and sophisticated
    "The Ivy League ideal is a gentleman or woman of culture, etiquette, wit, and an urbane manner."
    urbanus of a city

evacuate
    v. to remove from a place or area (to a safer place); to leave a place; to excrete waste matter from the body
    "An air pump is employed to evacuate a bell jar and create a vacuum."
    evacuation (n.)
    evacuatus (past participle of *evacuare* to empty out: *e-, ex-* out of + *vacuus* empty)

vacant
    adj. containing nothing; empty; unfilled; unoccupied; without activity
    "The movers left behind a house vacant of furnishings."
    vacatus (past participle of *vacare* to be empty, vacant, or idle)

evasive
    adj. inclined or intended to evade; intentionally vague or ambiguous
    "To avoid the oncoming truck, the driver swerved in an evasive maneuver."
    evadere to evade; to escape; to avoid: *e-, ex-* out of + *vadere* to go

invasion
    n. an instance of invading a country or region; an intrusion or encroachment
    "An invasion of locusts coupled with drought has led to widespread famine in Niger."
    invadere to enter; to attack: *in-* into + *vadere* to go

prevail	**v.** to be greater in strength or influence; to triumph, win out, or predominate "After whining and pleading, he prevailed on his dad to buy him an ice cream." *praevalere* to have greater strength or value: *prae-* before + *valere* to be strong
vindicate	**v.** to clear of accusation, blame, suspicion or doubt with supporting evidence or proof; to provide justification or support for; to defend, maintain, or insist on the recognition of one's rights; to avenge "Galileo's astronomical observations vindicated Copernicus's controversial theory." *vindication (n.)* *vindicatus* claimed; avenged (past participle of *vindicare* to claim; to avenge)
vindictive	**adj.** disposed to seek revenge; spiteful "The desire to get even is a vindictive response." *vindicatus* claimed; avenged (past participle of *vindicare* to claim; to avenge)
advent	**n.** a coming or arrival; the liturgical period preceding Christmas "The advent of a reliable chronometer allowed navigators to determine a ship's longitude." *advenire* to come to: *ad-* toward + *venire* to come
event	**n.** something that takes place; a social gathering or activity; the final result or outcome; a contest or item in a sports program "The outcomes of the roll of two dice comprise 36 possible random events." *evenire* to happen: *e-, ex-* out + *venire* to come.
vent	**v.** 1) to express one's thoughts or feelings "When she got home from work, she vented to her husband about her incompetent boss." **v.** 2) to release or discharge through an opening "The steam was vented through the pipe to avoid overheating." **n.** a means of escape or release from confinement; an opening or outlet permitting the escape of fumes, a liquid, a gas, or steam "In winter, you can see steam coming out of the dryer vent on the side of the house." *ventus* wind
verify	**v.** to prove the truth of something with evidence or testimony; to substantiate; to determine or test the truth or accuracy of by comparison or investigation; to affirm formally under oath "The predicted deflection of light during a solar eclipse verified Einstein's General Theory of Relativity." *verification (n.)* *verus* true + *facere* to make; to do
verity	**n.** the quality or state of being true, factual, or real; a true principal or belief "Ponce de Leon's quest for the Fountain of Youth showed he did not doubt its verity." *veritas* truth < *verus* true

verbal   **adj.** of, relating to, or associated with words; consisting of only words without action; spoken rather than written; oral
"Gestures, body language, and facial expressions are non-verbal forms of communication."
verbum word

verbose   **adj.** containing a great and usually an excessive number of words; wordy
"'Verbose', 'prolix,' and 'windy' are all synonyms descriptive of wordiness."
verbum word

adversity   **n.** a state of hardship or affliction
"Hannibal's elephants faced adversity in the form of snow and steep terrain when they crossed the Alps."
advertere to turn toward: *ad-* toward + *vertere* to turn

controversy   **n.** prolonged public disagreement or heated debate
"To postpone further controversy, the proposal to impose a dress code on the students was tabled."
controversial (adj.)
vertere to turn

diversion   **n.** the act or instance of diverting or turning aside; a distraction or deviation; something that distracts the mind and relaxes or entertains
"After a demanding day of work or school, many people find diversion in watching television."
divertere to divert: *di-, dis-* aside + *vertere* to turn

Exercise A

Use the word box at the beginning of the lesson to fill in the blanks below:

1. At the NASCAR _____, we cheered until we were hoarse.

2. The _____ of the personal computer revolutionized science, education, the workplace, and personal communication.

3. Academic language has a reputation for being _____.

4. Now that our children have all graduated from college, we're looking to move from our suburban home to an _____ condominium.

5. Each year when school gets out, we expect an _____ of tourists on Cape Cod.

6. Alex created a _____ to keep his mother occupied while Andrew stole the cookies from the cookie jar.

7. Our _____ agreement would not hold up in court: We need a written contract as well.

8. Even after we chatted for a while, he was _____ about sharing his investment strategy.

9. A _____ person usually harbors a grudge.

10. A congressional bill that would allow the FBI and CIA to tap American citizens' telephones without a warrant aroused a storm of _____.

11. The doctor expected the nurse to be _____ of the accusation that she administered an overdose.

12. She doubted the _____ of the story that the lion had befriended a lamb.

13. In the classic adventure story, the hero overcomes great _____ to reach his goal.

14. The environmental group mounted a protest when it learned the chemical plant was _____ toxic fumes.

15. The old _____ lot will become a community garden.

16. We hope to _____ on our members to contribute generously to our fund raising campaign.

17. To _____ his gold claim, he left his partner in charge and rode into the city to the assayer's office.

18. Whenever a hurricane is predicted, plans to _____ flood-prone areas are announced on the media.

19. The _____ English actor was noted for his elegant dinners at his winter retreat in the south of France.

Exercise B

Match the word with the letter of its definition:

1. ___ advent
2. ___ adversity
3. ___ controversy
4. ___ diversion
5. ___ evacuate
6. ___ evasive
7. ___ event
8. ___ invasion
9. ___ prevail
10. ___ urban
11. ___ urbane
12. ___ vacant
13. ___ vent
14. ___ verify
15. ___ verity
16. ___ verbal
17. ___ verbose
18. ___ vindicate
19. ___ vindictive

a) vague or elusive
b) to win
c) polite and sophisticated
d) prolonged or widespread disagreement
e) to remove; to clear out
f) empty; blank
g) wordy
h) arrival
i) vengeful
j) an influx
k) to confirm the truth of
l) oral
m) an occurrence; a competition
n) misfortune; difficulty
o) to acquit; to absolve
p) of a city
q) a duct allowing the passage of air or fumes
r) a distraction; a detour
s) truth

Exercise C

ACROSS
4 Wordy
6 To absolve
11 To win; to dominate
12 To remove; to clear out
14 A distraction
15 To release or discharge from an opening
16 To substantiate; to prove with evidence
17 Empty; blank
18 The truth; something that is accurate
19 A prolonged and widespread debate

DOWN
1 Elusive; vague
2 Sophisticated
3 From a city or populated area
5 Oral; said out loud rather than written
7 An influx; an attack
8 An arrival; the coming of something
9 Vengeful or spiteful
10 An occurrence; a competition
13 Misfortune

Lesson XXV

VIA, VID-, VIGIL-, VINC-, VIT-, VOC-, VOL-, VOLV-

VIA way	**VID-, VIS-** to see	**VIGIL-** to watch	**VINC-, VICT-** to conquer
VIT-, VIV- life	**VOC-, VOCAT-** to call	**VOL-** wish	**VOLV-, VOLUT-** to roll

> *deviate, devious, evidence, evident, improvise, invisible,*
> *supervise, visualize, surveillance, vigil, evict, invincible, victory,*
> *survival, advocate, vocation, voluntary, volition, evolve, revolve*

Word Definitions

deviate   v. to turn aside or cause to turn aside from a course or way; to depart from a norm; to stray
"A car that repeatedly deviates from its lane signals an impaired or distracted driver."
deviation (n.)
diviare to turn out of the way: *de-* away from + *via* way

devious   adj. not straightforward; shifty; departing from a correct or accepted way
"The devious wolf donned grandmother's clothes to hoodwink Red Riding Hood."
devius devious; retired; shy: *de-* away from + *via* way

evidence   n. a thing or things that are helpful in forming a conclusion or judgment; an outward sign; facts used for proof
"Defense attorneys often try to get judges to exclude evidence by arguing that it was obtained through an unconstitutional search."
evidens, evidentis obvious to the eye or mind: *e-, ex-* out + *videre* to see

evident   adj. easily seen or understood; plain or obvious; clear
"Something patently obvious and requiring no explanation is self-evident."
evidens, evidentis obvious to the eye or mind: *e-, ex-* out + *videre* to see

improvise   v. to invent, compose, or perform with little or no preparation; to do something extemporaneously; to make do without regular tools, materials, or income
"A prisoner improvised a rope from torn bed sheets to drop himself down the wall."
improvisation (n.)
im-, in- not + *providere* to foresee

invisible	**adj.** impossible to see; not accessible to view; hidden "The highway signs and lane markings rapidly became invisible as the fog rolled in." *invisibility (n.)* *in-* not + *videre* to see
supervise	**v.** to observe and direct the execution of "Eisenhower planned and supervised the D-Day invasion." *supervision (n.)* *supervidere* to survey; to supervise: *super-* over + *videre* to see
visualize	**v.** to form a mental image; to make visible "Daydreaming in his office cubicle, he visualized a romantic evening." *videre* to see
surveillance	**n.** the act of observing a person or group under suspicion "Surveillance cameras are mounted in stores to detect and discourage shoplifters." *vigilare* to keep awake; to watch < *vigil* awake; watchful
vigil	**n.** a period of staying awake during the time usually spent asleep, especially to watch or pray; a peaceful demonstration in support of a cause "Prior to the burial, mourners conducted a reverential vigil around the casket." *vigil* awake; watchful
evict	**v.** to expel someone from a property "The Pied Piper was hired by the town of Hamelin to evict the rats." *eviction (n.)* *evincere* to overcome; to defeat: *ex-* out + *vincere* to defeat
invincible	**adj.** incapable of being overcome or defeated; unconquerable "The supposedly invincible Maginot Line proved little deterrent to the invading Nazis. *invincibility (n.)* *in-* not + *vincere* to conquer
victory	**n.** the defeat of an enemy or opponent; success in a struggle against difficulties or an obstacle. *victorious (adj.)* "A Phyrric victory is one so costly that it is ruinous." *victoria* victory
survival	**n.** the act or process of remaining alive; the fact of having endured "*Robinson Crusoe* is a work of fiction based on the true story of Alexander Selkirk's survival as an island castaway." *supervivere* to survive; to outlive: *super-* above; in addition + *vivere* to live

advocate	**n.** a person who publicly supports or recommends a particular cause or policy; a person who pleads a case on someone else's behalf; a lawyer **v.** to recommend publicly or to support "A defense lawyer serves as advocate for the accused." *advocation (n.)* *advocare* to call to one's aid: *ad-* to + *vocare* to call
vocation	**n.** a person's employment or main occupation; a strong feeling of suitability for a particular career or occupation; a calling (especially religious) "Ben Franklin was a printer by vocation; invention was merely his avocation." *vocative (adj.)* *vocare* to call
voluntary	**adj.** done, given, or acting of one's own free will; working without payment "His work as head of the soccer association is completely voluntary." *voluntas* will
volition	**n.** the faculty or power of using one's own will "Depression often expresses itself in low energy and lack of volition." *volo* I want < *velle* to wish; to want
evolve	**v.** to develop or achieve gradually; the process of evolution (of species) "A worm evolves into a chrysalis from which a butterfly emerges." *evolution (n.), evolutionary (adj.)* *evolvere* to unroll: *ex-* out of + *volvere* to roll
revolve	**v.** (1) to orbit a central point; to turn on an axis; to rotate; to recur in cycles or periodically; to be centered **v.** (2) to treat as the center or most important element of "Over the course of a night, the visible stars seem to revolve around the North Star." *revolution (n.), revolutionary (adj.)* *revolvere* to turn over; to roll back: *re-* back; again + *volvere* to roll

Exercise A

Use the word box at the beginning of the lesson to fill in the blanks below:

1. What sets jazz musicians apart from their peers in other musical genres is their ability to
   _____.

2. Please, do not _____ from the architect's blueprint.

3. In graduate school, I continued to study philosophy of my own _____.

4. In the Christian Church, a _____ may be held the night before a festival or holy day.

5. The foreman's job is to _____ the line workers and make sure the machines are kept in good repair.

6. It is _____ that he is skilled at both analyzing and writing code; he quickly fixed several bugs that had bedeviled the other software engineers for weeks.

7. In the children's mystery story, the _____ ink on the back of the map could be made visible with a mild solution of lemon juice and water.

8. The hackers' _____ methods matched their unethical aims: to blackmail corporations into paying them to prevent denial-of-service attacks.

9. His _____ was dependent on his ability to evade the Mafia assassins.

10. We had a hard time _____ the wrinkled old lady as a once-famous beauty – until we saw her wedding photos.

11. In 2007, we celebrate the 100th anniversary of Rachel Carson, an early _____ for the environment who wrote about the devastating effects of DDT on the entire food chain.

12. Your attendance at the lecture is mandatory, but the T.A.'s discussion session is _____.

13. Our _____ at the homecoming game this year was even sweeter after last year's losing streak.

14. Charles Darwin scandalized the religious establishment with his claim that humans _____ from the great apes.

15. At the end of the month, the landlord always threatened to _____ any tenants who did not pay their rent on time.

16. Swordfishing on George's Bank is my _____.

17. When the weather is warm and humid, the fans over our beds _____ and keep us cool.

18. The prosecutor presented ample circumstantial _____ that he had committed the crime, so the jury convicted him.

19. Government _____ of our citizenry has greatly increased since the terrorist attacks of Sept. 11, 2001.

20. Children love superheroes because they are _____.

Exercise B
Match the word with the letter of its definition:

1. ___ advocate
2. ___ deviate
3. ___ devious
4. ___ evict
5. ___ evidence
6. ___ evident
7. ___ evolve
8. ___ improvise
9. ___ invincible
10. ___ invisible
11. ___ revolve
12. ___ supervise
13. ___ surveillance
14. ___ survival
15. ___ victory
16. ___ vigil
17. ___ visualize
18. ___ vocation
19. ___ volition
20. ___ voluntary

a) an occupation; a calling
b) obvious
c) to oust
d) a supporter or promoter
e) free will
f) to ad lib
g) invulnerable
h) the continued existence of (someone or something)
i) unable to be seen
j) to diverge from
k) a night watch
l) to develop slowly
m) sneaky; not straight
n) to oversee
o) optional
p) to rotate around a center
q) to envisage; to imagine
r) observation
s) facts or items of proof
t) success

Exercise C

ACROSS
2 The defeat of an enemy or opponent
3 To turn aside from a course or way; to depart from a norm
5 The act or process of remaining alive
6 Things or facts that are helpful in forming a conclusion or judgment
9 To perform with little or no preparation
14 To expel someone from a property
15 To form a mental image
16 Easily seen or understood; plain and obvious
17 A period of staying awake during the time usually spent asleep
18 A person's employment or main occupation
19 The act of observing a person or group under suspicion

DOWN
1 Shifty; departing from the correct or accepted way
4 Done of one's own free will
6 To develop or to achieve gradually
7 Impossible to see; hidden
8 To orbit a central point
10 Incapable of being overcome or defeated
11 The faculty or power of using one's own will
12 To observe and to direct the execution of
13 A person who publicly supports a particular cause or policy

Quiz 5

> *evacuate, controversy, stellar, vacant, invincible, victory, pertain, surveillance, constant, context, instruction, evident, event, turbid, improvise, devious, survival, aspire, spectators, dissolve, abundant, invisible, evolve*

1. In the _____ of an emergency, citizens must _____ their homes immediately.

2. The _____ over allowing gay men and lesbians to serve openly in the military has not ended, even with the repeal of "Don't ask, don't tell."

3. It was immediately _____ that the Driver's Education student was not ready to get behind the wheel, so the instructor had him practice on the simulator first.

4. After the team won its tenth straight _____ and moved into first place, the players' confidence and winning attitude made their team _____.

5. The sign outside the run-down motel always said "_____."

6. The Ukraine, once known as the "bread basket" of the Soviet Union for its _____ crops, was decimated: first by collective farming, and later by the Chernobyl nuclear disaster.

7. Although his contribution was interesting, it did not _____ to the topic.

8. Foreign language students often must rely on the _____ of a sentence or paragraph to decide which of several dictionary definitions applies to a particular use of a word.

9. His SAT scores were _____, helping earn him admission to Yale.

10. Cruise control keeps a driver's car at a _____ speed.

11. He _____ to play in the NBA, but his coaches gave him little formal _____.

12. Because of the widespread deployment of _____ cameras, even the most _____ robbers can no longer sneak around as though they were _____.

13. The ability to walk on two legs must have given the earliest humans a _____ advantage; therefore, we _____ to be exclusively bipedal.

14. The red clay partially _____ in the water, giving it a _____ appearance.

15. The _____ cheered after the saxophone player _____ a soul-stirring solo.

Answer Key

Lesson I

EXERCISE A

1. abduct
2. abhor
3. abrupt
4. absorb
5. abrasion
6. accord
7. adversary
8. adhered
9. adjacent
10. adaptable
11. ambiguous
12. ambidextrous
13. ante meridian
14. anticipate
15. benediction
16. bicuspid
17. bisected
18. bilateral
19. benefactor
20. bilingual

EXERCISE B

1. abduct — a. to carry off unlawfully
2. abhor — d. to detest
3. abrasion — c. the result of wearing away
4. abrupt — e. a sudden change in action or manner
5. absorb — b. to soak up
6. accord — g. an agreement
7. adaptable — j. able to adjust to new situations
8. adhere — h. to attach
9. adjacent — i. bordering
10. adversary — f. an opponent
11. ambidextrous — n. ability to use left and right hands equally
12. ambiguous — l. having more than one interpretation
13. ante meridian — k. before noon
14. anticipate — m. to expect
15. benediction — o. a blessing
16. benefactor — t. a person who offers financial support
17. bicuspid — p. a double pointed tooth
18. bilateral — q. having two sides
19. bilingual — r. the ability to speak two languages
20. bisect — s. to divide into two equal parts

Lesson II

EXERCISE A

1. contrast
2. contraband
3. circumscribed
4. contradicting
5. circulated
6. circumstantial
7. condone
8. collision
9. commiserate
10. collaborated
11. devoured
12. demented
13. demoted
14. deter
15. decadence
16. dedicated
17. distinct
18. duplicate
19. distortion
20. duet
21. distract

EXERCISE B

1. circulate — e. to move continuously or freely
2. circumscribe — f. to restrict
3. circumstantial — d. incidental; dependent on circumstances
4. collaborate — h. to work together on a project
5. collision — j. a crash
6. commiserate — i. to sympathize with the sorrow of another
7. condone — g. to excuse or forgive; to overlook
8. contraband — c. illegally imported or smuggled goods
9. contradict — a. to say the opposite of
10. contrast — b. striking difference in comparison
11. decadence — o. the process of moral or cultural decline
12. dedicate — p. to devote a creative work to a person
13. demented — m. mentally ill; wild and irrational
14. demote — l. to lower in rank or grade
15. deter — k. to discourage or prevent from occurring
16. devour — n. to consume voraciously
17. distortion — q. the action of twisting something out of shape
18. distract — s. to draw attention away from
19. duet — t. a performance by two entertainers
20. duplicate — r. to make an exact copy
21. distinct — u. different from something else

Lesson III

EXERCISE A

1. equivalent
2. emigrate
3. eradicated
4. evoke
5. equities
6. extroverts
7. illuminate
8. implicating
9. inclusive
10. inscription
11. illegible
12. irrelevant
13. illiterate
14. incessant
15. intersect
16. interlude
17. intravenous
18. introvert
19. intervene
20. interjection

EXERCISE B

1. equity   f. value of property after debts
2. equivalent   b. equal in all respects
3. emigrate   d. to leave one's country for another
4. eradicate   a. to get rid of entirely
5. evoke   c. to call forth
6. extrovert   e. an outgoing person
7. illuminate   h. to light up; to shed light on
8. implicate   g. to show to be involved in a crime
9. inclusive   i. including the limits specified
10. inscription   j. words written on a monument
11. illegible   m. difficult or impossible to read
12. illiterate   o. unable to read or write
13. incessant   n. continuing without interruption
14. irrelevant   p. off the subject
15. interjection   q. an exclamation
16. interlude   k. the time between two events
17. intersect   l. to cut across or through
18. intervene   s. to come between
19. intravenous   t. into vein(s)
20. introvert   r. a shy person

Lesson IV

EXERCISE A

1. magnificent
2. multilateral
3. major
4. malicious
5. magnitude
6. majority
7. multitude
8. obliterate
9. obsessing
10. obligation
11. persevere
12. perforated
13. perspective
14. omnivorous
15. postpone
16. prediction
17. preclude
18. presume
19. postscript
20. posterity

EXERCISE B

1. magnificent   e. spectacular; exceptional
2. magnitude   f. scope or importance
3. major   b. a rank in the army
4. majority   d. more than half of a group
5. malicious   g. intending to do harm
6. multilateral   c. involving three or more parties
7. multitude   a. a great throng of people or things
8. obligation   h. a duty
9. obliterate   i. to utterly destroy
10. obsess   j. to think about constantly
11. omnivorous   n. feeding on both plants and animals
12. perforate   l. to make a hole in; to pierce
13. persevere   k. to remain devoted to a difficult task
14. perspective   m. a point of view
15. posterity   p. future generations
16. postpone   o. to put off to a later time
17. postscript   t. an added note at the end of a letter
18. preclude   s. to make impossible; to prevent
19. prediction   r. a claim about future events
20. presume   q. to make an assumption

Lesson V

EXERCISE A

1. primary
2. primate
3. proceed
4. procession
5. provoke
6. profit
7. recite
8. reiterated
9. retrospect
10. recline
11. secluded
12. secure
13. supervised
14. suggested
15. suffocate
16. subscribe
17. unanimous
18. translucent
19. unity
20. transparent

EXERCISE B

1. primary   d. first in rank or importance
2. primate   a. humans, gorillas, and monkeys
3. proceed   e. to begin a course of action
4. procession   b. a parade
5. profit   c. to benefit financially
6. provoke   f. to deliberately annoy or anger
7. recite   i. to repeat by memory
8. recline   j. to lean back or lie down
9. reiterate   g. to say again
10. retrospect   h. a review of past events
11. seclude   n. to remove from social interaction; to isolate
12. secure   k. to protect against threats
13. supervise   m. to oversee
14. subscribe   p. to arrange to receive periodically
15. suffocate   o. to make unable to breathe
16. suggest   l. to put forward for consideration
17. translucent   r. allowing light to pass through partially
18. transparent   s. see-through
19. unanimous   t. completely in agreement
20. unity   q. oneness

Lesson VI

EXERCISE A

1. acrid
2. alias
3. agility
4. altitude
5. acute
6. agitate
7. alienate
8. alter
9. aliens
10. agriculture
11. annual
12. inept
13. animosity
14. animate
15. amateur
16. aptitude
17. aperture
18. annuity
19. amiable
20. ambulatory

EXERCISE B

1. acrid   g. pungent and bitter
2. acute   l. very perceptive
3. agility   b. nimbleness
4. agitate   n. to disturb
5. agriculture   h. farming
6. alias   o. a false label or name
7. alien   c. foreign
8. alienate   p. to estrange
9. alter   d. to change
10. altitude   e. height from the ground or sea level
11. amateur   q. a non-professional
12. amiable   t. friendly
13. ambulatory   k. able to walk; mobile
14. animate   f. to bring to life; to inspire
15. animosity   j. a strong hostility
16. annual   a. yearly
17. annuity   r. a yearly payment of money
18. aperture   m. an opening
19. aptitude   s. a natural ability
20. inept   i. incompetent

Lesson VII

EXERCISE A

1. beatitude
2. battery
3. audible
4. army
5. audience
6. artifacts
7. artificial
8. avuncular
9. auditorium
10. casualty
11. abbreviation
12. candid
13. rebellious
14. brevity
15. candidate
16. incantation
17. imbibe
18. recalcitrant
19. capture
20. participated

EXERCISE B

1. abbreviation   g. a shortened form of a word
2. army   m. an organized military force
3. artifact   a. a man-made object
4. artificial   t. unnatural
5. audible   i. able to be heard
6. audience   o. spectators
7. auditorium   c. a theater or hall
8. avuncular   q. kindly, like an uncle
9. battery   e. injury purposely inflicted on someone else
10. beatitude   k. supreme blessedness or happiness
11. brevity   d. the quality of being concise
12. casualty   n. a person or thing killed or injured, usually in war
13. candid   b. honest and frank
14. candidate   s. a job applicant or nominated official
15. capture   f. to control by force
16. imbibe   l. to drink
17. incantation   j. a magic spell
18. participate   h. to take part in
19. rebellious   p. unmanageable
20. recalcitrant   r. obstinate

Lesson VIII

EXERCISE A

1. carnivorous
2. discernment
3. decapitate
4. castigated
5. cerebral
6. access
7. census
8. accessories
9. decelerates
10. censor
11. accelerate
12. incision
13. century
14. incited
15. civilian
16. concise
17. centennial
18. civilization
19. excite
20. civil

EXERCISE B

1. access — f. to approach or enter
2. accessory — j. a supplementary item
3. accelerate — p. to speed up
4. carnivorous — a. eating only meat
5. castigate — i. to reprimand severely
6. censor — b. someone who monitors and suppresses unacceptable speech
7. census — q. an official count of population
8. cerebral — l. of the brain; intellectual
9. centennial — c. one hundredth anniversary
10. century — m. a period of one hundred years
11. civil — d. relating to ordinary citizens (not military)
12. civilian — o. someone not in the military
13. civilization — e. an advanced system of human development
14. concise — s. expressed clearly and in few words
15. decapitate — n. to cut off the head
16. decelerate — r. to slow down
17. discernment — g. the ability to make fine distinctions
18. excite — t. to arouse; to awaken
19. incision — h. a surgical cut
20. incite — k. to stir up or cause to act

Lesson IX

EXERCISE A

1. cloister
2. clarify
3. clarity
4. acclaim
5. closure
6. enclosure
7. inclined
8. decline
9. comply
10. copious
11. accolades
12. complement
13. cognition
14. incognito
15. cordial
16. incorporate
17. creed
18. corpses
19. credible
20. recluse

EXERCISE B

1. acclaim — j. praise
2. accolade — n. a high honor
3. clarify — g. to separate out the impurities; to clear up
4. clarity — k. transparency
5. cloister — e. a covered walkway; to seclude in an abbey or monastery
6. closure — p. a feeling of resolution
7. cognition — h. the process of thinking
8. complement — l. to fit well with something else
9. comply — d. to meet specified standards
10. copious — r. abundant
11. cordial — c. warm and friendly
12. corpse — i. a dead body
13. credible — m. competent, but not outstanding
14. creed — b. articles of faith
15. decline — a. to decrease; to refuse
16. enclosure — t. something placed in an envelope with a letter
17. inclined — s. leaning toward (something)
18. incognito — f. anonymously
19. incorporate — o. to take in; to include
20. recluse — q. a hermit

Lesson X

EXERCISE A

1. crescendo
2. succumb
3. culpable
4. cruciform
5. incumbent
6. Cupid
7. accrue
8. docile
9. mandate
10. curriculum
11. trident
12. data
13. concur
14. indentation
15. domestic
16. domain
17. dominant
18. diction
19. verdict
20. dictator

EXERCISE B

1. accrue
2. concur
3. crescendo
4. cruciform
5. culpable
6. cupidity
7. curriculum
8. data
9. dictator
10. diction
11. docile
12. domain
13. domestic
14. dominant
15. incumbent
16. indentation
17. mandate
18. succumb
19. trident
20. verdict

e. to increase or add to over time
j. to agree
m. a steady increase in volume
f. shaped like a cross
s. deserving blame
p. an extreme desire for riches
i. a course of study
k. information for analysis
q. an absolute ruler
b. manner or clarity of speech
o. submissive
c. an area under control
g. a household servant
a. controlling; most powerful
n. the current holder of a public office or post
h. the space set in from the margin of a document
l. to demand action
r. to yield; to give in to
d. a three-pronged weapon
t. a jury's decision

Lesson XI

EXERCISE A

1. egocentric
2. equal
3. dormant
4. erratic
5. erroneous
6. endorsed
7. façade
8. fervor
9. facsimile
10. deface
11. infallible
12. fiction
13. falsify
14. affinity
15. fidelity
16. conferred
17. finite
18. fertile
19. figurative
20. configuration

EXERCISE B

1. affinity
2. confer
3. configuration
4. deface
5. dormant
6. egocentric
7. endorse
8. equal
9. erratic
10. erroneous
11. facade
12. facsimile
13. falsify
14. fervor
15. fertile
16. fiction
17. fidelity
18. figurative
19. finite
20. infallible

k. natural preference
n. to consult with
f. an arrangement or pattern
e. to disfigure
q. asleep or inactive
d. self-centered
h. to publicly support
p. having the same value
m. irregular
b. incorrect
s. an illusion
g. a duplicate
c. to alter so as to mislead or make false
a. heightened passion
t. capable of supporting abundant life
i. prose literature that is not factual
r. loyalty
l. using figures of speech
j. having a limit
o. foolproof

Lesson XII

EXERCISE A

1. fluid
2. floral
3. confirmed
4. deflect
5. infirmary
6. fragile
7. forum
8. inflection
9. fugitive
10. fortunate
11. fraternal
12. fragments
13. confronted
14. diffuse
15. fusion
16. gorge
17. genre
18. generous
19. genuine
20. generate

EXERCISE B

1. confirm   k. to acknowledge the truth of
2. confront   b. to face
3. diffuse   g. to spread over a wide area
4. deflect   l. to turn (something) aside
5. floral   m. consisting of or relating to flowers
6. fluid   c. a shapeless substance; a liquid or gas
7. fortunate   h. favored by good luck
8. forum   f. a place for discussion
9. fragment   a. a piece of a whole
10. fragile   o. easily breakable
11. fraternal   n. brotherly
12. fugitive   d. a person who flees from the law
13. fusion   s. a joining together
14. generate   e. to cause to exist
15. generous   j. freely giving
16. genre   t. a category
17. genuine   r. authentic
18. gorge   i. a steep valley; to eat greedily
19. inflection   p. the modulation of intonation in the voice
20. infirmary   q. a hospital within a larger institution

Lesson XIII

EXERCISE A

1. congregation
2. junction
3. inherent
4. gratitude
5. prejudice
6. itinerary
7. graduation
8. ingredient
9. inject
10. juncture
11. irate
12. incense
13. progress
14. projectile
15. impelled
16. transition
17. transit
18. jocular
19. gradual
20. congratulation

EXERCISE B

1. congratulation — h. acknowledgement and approval
2. congregation — m. a gathering of people; a religious flock
3. impel — b. to drive toward
4. gradual — g. taking place in stages over a period of time
5. graduate — l. to complete a diploma or degree
6. gratitude — n. thankfulness
7. ingredient — k. a component
8. inherent — p. permanent or essential (of a characteristic or attribute)
9. incense — d. to infuriate
10. inject — o. to force liquid into something
11. irate — c. extremely angry
12. itinerary — f. a planned route
13. jocular — r. humorous
14. junction — t. an intersection of two roads or rail lines
15. juncture — a. a critical point in time
16. prejudice — i. a preconceived idea or bias
17. progress — q. to move forward
18. projectile — s. a missile; something propelled with force
19. transit — j. the act of passing from one place to another
20. transition — e. the process of changing

Lesson XIV

EXERCISE A

1. eloquent
2. League
3. deluge
4. liberal
5. legitimate
6. locality
7. delegate
8. legacy
9. collateral
10. colloquial
11. levity
12. liberty
13. delusions
14. lingual
15. literal
16. illuminate
17. laborious
18. elusive
19. license
20. lucid

EXERCISE B

1. collateral
2. colloquial
3. delegate
4. delusion
5. deluge
6. eloquent
7. elusive
8. illuminate
9. laborious
10. legitimate
11. levity
12. league
13. legacy
14. liberal
15. liberty
16. license
17. lingual
18. literal
19. locality
20. lucid

k. something pledged as security for a loan
d. familiar and conversational speech
j. to entrust to someone
p. an unrealistic idea or belief
q. to flood or inundate
a. articulate and expressive
r. difficult to find or achieve
e. to shed light on
i. requiring considerable time and effort
n. conforming to the law
f. lighthearted or humorous speech
s. a union of persons or countries
c. something bequeathed at death
l. having or giving freely
b. freedom
t. a permit or official permission
g. relating to the tongue
m. straightforward; using the exact words
h. an area or specific site
o. clear

Lesson XV

EXERCISE A

1. manufacture
2. immersion
3. mediocre
4. minimal
5. medieval
6. motion
7. promise
8. manipulate
9. memorabilia
10. matrimony
11. memory
12. merge
13. maternal
14. missile
15. moment
16. mandatory
17. maritime
18. mend
19. momentum
20. minimize

EXERCISE B

1. immersion — j. covering completely with liquid
2. manipulate — f. to cleverly control or influence, especially for one's own benefit
3. mandatory — r. required
4. manufacture — m. to fabricate
5. maritime — l. relating to the sea
6. maternal — b. related through one's mother
7. matrimony — n. the rite of marriage
8. medieval — e. belonging to the Middle Ages
9. mediocre — i. of average quality
10. memorabilia — t. objects kept in association with memorable events
11. memory — d. the mental faculty of retaining information
12. mend — q. to restore to a sound condition
13. merge — h. to combine into a single entity
14. minimal — g. the least possible
15. minimize — o. to reduce to the least possible amount
16. missile — a. a projectile
17. moment — k. a very brief period of time
18. momentum — s. the impetus gained by a moving object
19. motion — c. the action or process of moving
20. promise — p. a binding statement of intent

Lesson XVI

EXERCISE A

1. native
2. immortal
3. mountain
4. innovation
5. mortify
6. commute
7. navigated
8. nocturnal
9. novelty
10. announce
11. mutates
12. mustered
13. negate
14. annihilate
15. monitor
16. Naval
17. nominal
18. negative
19. morality
20. novice

EXERCISE B

1. annihilate   k. to destroy completely
2. announce   d. to make known publicly
3. commute   b. to travel a certain distance regularly
4. immortal   s. living forever
5. innovation   p. a new method, idea, or product
6. monitor   t. to observe over time
7. morality   e. a set of principles of conduct
8. mortify   m. to humiliate
9. mountain   o. a conical, natural elevation of the earth's surface
10. muster   o. to gather together
11. mutate   f. to undergo a change or alteration
12. naval   g. relating to ships
13. native   j. original to a particular person or place
14. navigate   r. to travel on a desired course
15. negate   i. to invalidate
16. negative   n. a contradiction, denial, or refusal
17. nocturnal   a. active at night
18. nominal   q. symbolic or minimal; existing in name only
19. novelty   c. something new and/or unusual
20. novice   l. an inexperienced person

Lesson XVII

EXERCISE A

1. patron
2. operate
3. pacify
4. ostentatious
5. repast
6. passionate
7. ordain
8. impeccable
9. pedestrian
10. olfactory
11. pedal
12. oculist
13. orbit
14. odious
15. patriotism
16. orator
17. pendant
18. ornate
19. propeller
20. pecuniary

EXERCISE B

1. impeccable
2. oculist
3. odious
4. olfactory
5. operate
6. orator
7. orbit
8. ordain
9. ornate
10. ostentatious
11. pacify
12. passionate
13. patriotism
14. patron
15. pecuniary
16. pedal
17. pedestrian
18. pendant
19. propeller
20. repast

j. faultless
n. one who treats eye diseases
e. hateful; extremely unpleasant
s. relating to the sense of smell
b. to manage or function
r. a proficient public speaker
c. the rotation of a smaller heavenly body around a larger one
k. to appoint officially
l. highly decorated
a. characterized by pretentious display
f. to make quiet; to bring peace
o. having or showing powerful emotions
d. strong support for one's country
i. a person who gives financial support
g. relating to money
h. a foot-operated lever or control
m. a person traveling by foot
p. a suspended ornament
t. a fan-like device that drives an aircraft or boat
q. a meal

Lesson XVIII

EXERCISE A

1. potable
2. predatory
3. reprisal
4. postpone
5. placid
6. pittance
7. depict
8. opportune
9. proponent
10. potion
11. impotent
12. portable
13. apprehend
14. pontiff
15. potential
16. petition
17. ponderous
18. imposter
19. piety
20. appetite

EXERCISE B

1. appetite — k. an instinctive physical desire, especially hunger
2. apprehend — i. to arrest for a crime; to perceive
3. depict — d. to show through an art form
4. imposter — h. someone using a false identity
5. impotent — n. helpless; powerless
6. opportune — q. especially convenient or appropriate
7. petition — b. a formal request
8. piety — j. reverence; devotion to God
9. pittance — e. a very small amount of money
10. placid — r. calm; peaceful
11. ponderous — a. weighty; heavy
12. pontiff — c. the Pope
13. portable — o. easily carried or moved
14. postpone — t. to put off until later
15. potable — s. drinkable
16. potential — p. capacity to develop for the future
17. potion — g. a liquid mixture with magical, healing, or poisonous properties
18. predatory — m. preying on others
19. proponent — f. an advocate
20. reprisal — l. an act of retaliation

Lesson XIX

EXERCISE A

1. ratio
2. rapture
3. interrupt
4. regular
5. oppress
6. arrogant
7. rotate
8. rupture
9. rationale
10. compute
11. amputate
12. interrogative
13. ridicule
14. rectify
15. pungent
16. rational
17. interrogate
18. punish
19. derogatory
20. rector
21. derided

EXERCISE B

1. amputate
2. arrogant
3. compute
4. derogatory
5. interrogate
6. interrogative
7. interrupt
8. oppress
9. pungent
10. punish
11. rapture
12. ratio
13. rational
14. rationale
15. rectify
16. rector
17. regular
18. ridicule
19. rotate
20. rupture
21. deride

g. to cut off a limb or digit
p. having an exaggerated sense of one's importance
i. to determine by mathematics
j. critical and disrespectful
e. to question aggressively
h. questioning
m. to disturb; to halt something
o. to keep down unjustly
l. strong and unpleasant to the smell or taste
c. to inflict a penalty for a wrong
r. intense joy
f. a quantitative relationship between two amounts
b. sensible; logical
n. a logical basis for a belief or course of action
a. to put right
d. the priest in charge of a church
s. arranged in a consistent pattern; occurring at consistent intervals
q. to mock
k. to move in a circle around an axis
u. to burst suddenly
t. to speak of someone with scorn

Lesson XX

EXERCISE A

1. dissect
2. assault
3. sensory
4. saline
5. sacred
6. prescribe
7. consensus
8. consecutive
9. senile
10. sequence
11. manuscript
12. sacrament
13. session
14. resent
15. sanguine
16. consequence
17. sequel
18. segment
19. assailed
20. satiate

EXERCISE B

1. assail
2. assault
3. consensus
4. consecutive
5. consequence
6. dissect
7. manuscript
8. prescribe
9. resent
10. sacrament
11. sacred
12. saline
13. sanguine
14. satiate
15. segment
16. senile
17. sensory
18. sequel
19. sequence
20. session

j. to attack
e. a physical attack or threat of harm
l. a general agreement
q. successive; following immediately after
t. the result of an action
h. to analyze in minute detail
b. a handwritten book, document, or piece of music
d. to write a prescription; to advise
n. to hold a grudge
i. a religious ceremony invoking divine grace
m. religious; holy
g. salty in nature
a. cheerfully optimistic
r. to satisfy to the full
f. to divide into separate pieces; a piece
s. mentally feeble due to old age
k. relating to sensation or the physical senses
c. a follow up in a series
p. a particular order
o. a meeting

Lesson XXI

EXERCISE A

1. perspective
2. absolute
3. aspersion
4. disperse
5. simultaneous
6. resolution
7. simulate
8. despicable
9. dissolve
10. insomnia
11. solitude
12. resonate
13. simile
14. supersonic
15. spectacle
16. solo
17. resolve
18. spectator
19. Sonar
20. spectrum

EXERCISE B

1. absolute   f. complete and total
2. aspersion   k. an attack on one's reputation
3. despicable   b. contemptible
4. dissolve   j. to disappear, deteriorate, or degenerate; to disperse in a liquid
5. disperse   i. to distribute or spread over a wide area
6. insomnia   m. inability to sleep
7. perspective   g. point of view
8. resolution   p. a firm decision
9. resolve   c. to settle; to decide
10. resonate   q. to reverberate with sound
11. simile   d. a figure of speech comparing one thing to another
12. simulate   o. to imitate an appearance or action
13. simultaneous   a. at the same time
14. solitude   n. the state of being alone
15. solo   r. done by one person alone
16. sonar   h. an echolocation system
17. spectacle   s. a fantastic visual display or exhibition
18. spectator   l. an audience member; a bystander
19. spectrum   t. a range
20. supersonic   e. faster than the speed of sound

Lesson XXII

EXERCISE A

1. tangible
2. obstruct
3. contemporary
4. aspire
5. constant
6. presume
7. constricted
8. spiritual
9. temperaments
10. stellar
11. respiratory
12. temper
13. construct
14. Temporal
15. conspiracy
16. tangent
17. suave
18. constellations
19. instruct

EXERCISE B

1. aspire — g. to hope to accomplish
2. conspiracy — k. a secret plot involving more than one person
3. constant — m. unchanging
4. constellation — f. a group of stars
5. constrict — o. to make narrower
6. construct — e. to build; to erect
7. contemporary — p. modern
8. instruct — l. to teach
9. obstruct — j. to block
10. presume — b. to suppose
11. respiratory — q. affecting breathing or respiration
12. spiritual — c. nonmaterial; religious
13. stellar — a. involving the stars
14. suave — r. charming and elegant
15. tangent — h. a line that touches a curve at one point
16. tangible — d. touchable
17. temper — s. a fit of rage
18. temperament — n. disposition
19. temporal — i. secular; material

Lesson XXIII

EXERCISE A

1. Mediterranean
2. ultimatum
3. distort
4. extraterrestrial
5. pertinent
6. context
7. ultimate
8. totalitarian
9. subterranean
10. abundant
11. terrain
12. intrude
13. terminate
14. detract
15. pertain
16. corrupt
17. redundant
18. contort
19. extract
20. turbid

EXERCISE B

1. abundant — f. plentiful
2. context — j. frame of reference
3. contort — e. to twist
4. corrupt — m. dishonest; unethical
5. detract — i. to belittle
6. distort — n. to pull out of shape
7. extract — b. to pull out; to remove
8. extraterrestrial — o. alien; originating outside the earth and its atmosphere
9. intrude — k. to enter without permission
10. Mediterranean — a. characteristic of the Mediterranean Sea
11. pertain — p. to relate to
12. pertinent — d. relevant
13. redundant — q. unnecessary; repetitive
14. subterranean — t. below the earth's surface
15. terminate — g. to bring to an end
16. terrain — h. a stretch of land; surface characteristics of the land
17. totalitarian — l. autocratic
18. turbid — s. murky
19. ultimate — r. eventual; final
20. ultimatum — c. a final statement of terms

Lesson XXIV

EXERCISE A

1. event
2. advent
3. verbose
4. urban
5. invasion
6. diversion
7. verbal
8. evasive
9. vindictive
10. controversy
11. vindicated
12. verity
13. adversity
14. venting
15. vacant
16. prevail
17. verify
18. evacuate
19. urbane

EXERCISE B

1. advent   h. arrival
2. adversity   n. misfortune; difficulty
3. controversy   d. prolonged or widespread disagreement
4. diversion   r. a distraction; a detour
5. evacuate   e. to remove; to clear out
6. evasive   a. vague or elusive
7. event   m. an occurrence; a competition
8. invasion   j. an influx
9. prevail   b. to win
10. urban   p. of a city
11. urbane   c. polite and sophisticated
12. vacant   f. empty; blank
13. vent   q. a duct allowing the passage of air or fumes
14. verify   k. to confirm the truth of
15. verity   s. truth
16. verbal   l. oral
17. verbose   g. wordy
18. vindicate   o. to acquit; to absolve
19. vindictive   i. vengeful

Lesson XXV

EXERCISE A

1. improvise
2. deviate
3. volition
4. vigil
5. supervise
6. evident
7. invisible
8. devious
9. survival
10. visualizing
11. advocate
12. voluntary
13. victory
14. evolve
15. evict
16. vocation
17. revolve
18. evidence
19. surveillance
20. invincible

EXERCISE B

1. advocate — d. a supporter or promoter
2. deviate — j. to diverge from
3. devious — m. sneaky; not straight
4. evict — c. to oust
5. evidence — s. facts or items of proof
6. evident — b. obvious
7. evolve — l. to develop slowly
8. improvise — f. to ad lib
9. invincible — g. invulnerable
10. invisible — i. unable to be seen
11. revolve — p. to rotate around a center
12. supervise — n. to oversee
13. surveillance — r. observation
14. survival — h. the continued existence of (someone or something)
15. victory — t. success
16. vigil — k. a night watch
17. visualize — q. to envisage; to imagine
18. vocation — a. an occupation; a calling
19. volition — e. free will
20. voluntary — o. optional

Quizzes

Quiz 1

1. anticipated
2. retrospect
3. condone
4. multitude
5. provoke
6. obliterate, eradicate
7. unity
8. postponed, imminent
9. demote
10. evoke
11. abhor
12. magnificent, secluded
13. emigrated, bilingual
14. interjections, irrelevant
15. intersection

Quiz 2

1. civilians
2. verdict
3. copious
4. artifacts
5. alienated, amiable
6. acute, corpses, acrid
7. recluse, incorporate
8. civilization
9. amateur, agility
10. annuity
11. aptitude
12. agitate, carnivorous
13. crescendo
14. incumbent
15. inept

Quiz 3

1. transition
2. irate
3. legacy
4. fragile, fortunate
5. fertile, defaced
6. fragment
7. lucid
8. genuine, levity
9. mandatory, immersion
10. progress, elusive
11. mediocre
12. dormant
13. congregation, incense
14. liberal
15. elusive

Quiz 4

1. mustered, mountain
2. annihilated
3. proponent
4. opportune
5. placid
6. potential, impeccable
7. amputate
8. oppress, punish
9. ridiculed
10. derogatory, interrupted
11. Sacraments, sacred
12. consecutive, sanguine
13. consensus
14. consequence, resented

Quiz 5

1. event, evacuate
2. controversy
3. evident
4. victory, invincible
5. vacant
6. abundant
7. pertain
8. context
9. stellar
10. constant
11. aspired, instruction
12. surveillance, devious, invisible
13. survival, evolved
14. dissolved, turbid
15. spectators, improvised

Index

abbreviation, 44
abduct, 7
abhor, 7
abrasion, 7
abrupt, 7
absolute, 130
absorb, 7
abundant, 143
accelerate, 50
access, 50
accessory, 50
acclaim, 55
accolade, 56
accord, 7
accrue, 61
acrid, 37
acute, 37
adaptable, 7
adhere, 8
adjacent, 8
advent, 148
adversary, 8
adversity, 149
affinity, 70
agility, 37
agitate, 37
agriculture, 37
alias, 38
alien, 38
alienate, 38
alter, 38
altitude, 38
amateur, 38
ambidextrous, 8
ambiguous, 8
ambulatory, 38
amiable, 38
amputate, 116
animate, 38
animosity, 38
annihilate, 100
announce, 100
annual, 39

annuity, 39
ante meridian, 8
anticipate, 8
aperture, 39
appetite, 110
apprehend, 112
aptitude, 39
army, 43
arrogant, 118
artifact, 43
artificial, 43
aspersion, 131
aspire, 135
assail, 122
assault, 122
audible, 43
audience, 43
auditorium, 43
avuncular, 44
battery, 44
beatitude, 44
benediction, 8
benefactor, 8
bicuspid, 9
bilateral, 9
bilingual, 9
bisect, 9
brevity, 44
candid, 44
candidate, 45
capture, 45
carnivorous, 49
castigate, 49
casualty, 44
censor, 50
census, 50
centennial, 50
century, 51
cerebral, 49
circulate, 13
circumscribe, 13
circumstantial, 13
civil, 51

civilian, 51
civilization, 51
clarify, 55
clarity, 55
cloister, 55
closure, 56
cognition, 56
collaborate, 13
collateral, 86
collision, 13
colloquial, 88
commiserate, 13
commute, 99
complement, 56
comply, 57
compute, 116
concise, 51
concur, 62
condone, 13
confer, 69
configuration, 70
confirm, 74
confront, 75
congratulation(s), 81
congregation, 81
consecutive, 123
consensus, 124
consequence, 123
conspiracy, 135
constant, 135
constellation, 136
constrict, 136
construct, 136
contemporary, 137
context, 142
contort, 142
contraband, 14
contradict, 14
contrast, 14
controversy, 149
copious, 57
cordial, 57
corpse, 57
corrupt, 143
creditable, 57
creed, 57
crescendo, 61
cruciform, 61
culpable, 62

cupidity, 62
curriculum, 62
data, 62
decadence, 14
decapitate, 49
decelerate, 50
decline, 56
dedicate, 14
deface, 69
deflect, 74
delegate, 87
deluge, 86
delusion, 88
demented, 14
demote, 14
depict, 110
deride, 117
derogatory, 118
despicable, 131
deter, 14
detract, 142
deviate, 153
devious, 153
devour, 14
dictator, 62
diction, 62
diffuse, 75
discernment, 49
disperse, 131
dissect, 123
dissolve, 130
distinct, 14
distort, 142
distortion, 15
distract, 15
diversion, 149
docile, 63
domain, 63
domestic, 63
dominant, 63
dormant, 68
duet, 15
duplicate, 15
egocentric, 68
eloquent, 88
elusive, 88
emigrate, 19
enclosure, 56
endorse, 68

equal, 68
equity, 19
equivalent, 19
eradicate, 19
erratic, 69
erroneous, 69
evacuate, 147
evasive, 147
event, 148
evidence, 153
evident, 153
evoke, 19
excite, 51
extract, 143
extraterrestrial, 141
extrovert, 19
façade, 69
facsimile, 69
falsify, 69
fertile, 69
fervor, 69
fiction, 69
fidelity, 70
figurative, 70
finite, 70
floral, 74
fluid, 75
fortunate, 75
forum, 75
fragment, 75
fraternal, 75
fugitive, 75
fusion, 76
generate, 76
generous, 76
genre, 76
genuine, 76
gorge, 76
gradual, 80
graduate, 80
gratitude, 81
illegible, 20
illiterate, 20
illuminate, 20, 88
imbibe, 44
immersion, 93
immortal, 98
impeccable, 106
impel, 81

implicate, 20
imposter, 111
impotent, 111
improvise, 153
incantation, 45
incense, 81
incessant, 20
incision, 51
incite, 51
inclined, 56
inclusive, 20
incognito, 56
incorporate, 57
incumbent, 61
indentation, 62
inept, 39
infallible, 69
infirmary, 74
inflection, 74
ingredient, 80
inherent, 81
inject, 82
innovation, 100
inscription, 20
insomnia, 130
instruct, 136
interjection, 20
interlude, 20
interrogate, 118
interrogative, 118
interrupt, 118
intersect, 20
intervene, 21
intravenous, 21
introvert, 21
intrude, 143
invasion, 147
invisible, 154
irate, 81
irrelevant, 20
itinerary, 81
jocular, 82
junction, 82
juncture, 82
laborious, 86
league, 87
legacy, 86
legitimate, 86
levity, 87

liberal, 87
liberty, 87
license, 87
lingual, 87
literal, 87
locality, 87
lucid, 88
magnificent, 24
magnitude, 24
major, 24
majority, 24
malicious, 24
mandate, 62
mandatory, 92
manipulate, 92
manufacture, 92
manuscript, 123
maritime, 92
maternal, 92
matrimony, 92
medieval, 92
mediocre, 93
mediterranean, 141
memorabilia, 93
memory, 93
mend, 93
merge, 93
minimal, 93
minimize, 93
missile, 93
moment, 94
momentum, 94
monitor, 98
morality, 98
mortify, 99
motion, 94
mountain, 98
multilateral, 24
multitude, 25
muster, 98
mutate, 99
native, 99
naval, 99
negate, 99
negative, 99
nocturnal, 100
nominal, 100
novelty, 100
novice, 100

obligation, 25
obliterate, 25
obsess, 25
obstruct, 136
oculist, 104
odious, 104
olfactory, 104
omnivorous, 25
operate, 104
opportune, 111
oppress, 116
orator, 104
orbit, 105
ordain, 105
ornament, 105
ornate, 105
ostentatious, 105
pacify, 106
participate, 45
passionate, 105
patriotism, 105
patron, 105
pecuniary, 106
pedal, 106
pedestrian, 106
pendant, 106
perforate, 25
persevere, 25
perspective, 25, 131
pertain, 141
pertinent, 141
petition, 110
piety, 110
pittance, 110
placid, 111
ponderous, 111
pontiff, 111
portable, 111
posterity, 25
postpone, 26, 111
postscript, 26
potable, 111
potential, 111
potion, 112
preclude, 26
predatory, 112
prediction, 26
prejudice, 82
prescribe, 123

presume, 26, 136
prevail, 148
primary, 30
primate, 30
proceed, 30
procession, 30
profit, 30
progress, 80
projectile, 82
promise, 93
propeller, 106
proponent, 111
provoke, 30
pungent, 116
punish, 116
rapture, 117
ratio, 117
rational, 117
rationale, 117
rebellious, 44
recalcitrant, 44
recite, 31
recline, 31
recluse, 56
rectify, 117
rector, 117
redundant, 144
regular, 117
reiterate, 31
repast, 105
reprisal, 112
resent, 124
resolution, 130
resolve, 130
resonate, 130
respiratory, 135
retrospect, 31
ridicule, 117
rotate, 118
rupture, 118
sacrament, 122
sacred, 122
saline, 122
sanguine, 123
satiate, 123
seclude, 31
secure, 31
segment, 123
senile, 124

sensory, 124
sequel, 123
sequence, 124
session, 124
simile, 129
simulate, 129
simultaneous, 129
solitude, 129
solo, 129
sonar, 130
spectacle, 131
spectator, 131
spectrum, 131
spiritual, 135
stellar, 136
suave, 136
subscribe, 31
subterranean, 142
succumb, 61
suffocate, 31
suggest, 31
supersonic, 130
supervise, 32
tangent, 137
tangible, 137
temper, 137
temperament, 137
temporal, 137
terminate, 141
terrain, 142
totalitarian, 142
transit, 82
transition, 81
translucent, 32
transparent, 32
trident, 62
turbid, 143
ultimate, 143
ultimatum, 143
unanimous, 32
unity, 32
urban, 147
urbane, 147
vacant, 147
vent, 148
verbal, 149
verbose, 149
verdict, 63
verify, 148

verity, 148
vindicate, 148

vindictive, 148

www.ingramcontent.com/pod-product-compliance
Lightning Source LLC
Chambersburg PA
CBHW060314240426
43661CB00059B/2762